In an age filled with skepticism a
reminds believers that positive and
book is a must-read for those who th
or even one's own usefulness is simp

—Dr. John Fozard

President, Mid-America Christian University, Oklahoma City

Impact: That'll Leave a Mark *is a timely book about the practical yet profound effect of God's people on the culture they serve. Dr. Pratt encourages us to "go be the Body—everywhere, to everyone, all the time." Embracing the principles of truth and pragmatic approach found here will help release you into the realm of impact as a follower of Jesus and challenge the church to take a new look at its ministry and mission.*

—Mitchell Burch

Pastor/Evangelist and Church Consultant

Dr. Melissa Pratt brings uncommon courage, insight, and conviction to a broad range of situations faced by Christians and congregations when responding to contemporary values and culture. This book is a practical and powerful resource for equipping followers of Jesus in all walks of life to acquire a sustainable Christian witness for maximum impact in our time.

—Dr. Cheryl J. Sanders

Senior Pastor, Third Street Church of God, Washington, D.C.

Jesus famously called his followers to become "salt and light." These are the two drivers of Christian ministry, bringing influence that changes the taste, tenor, and perspective of everything (and everyone) it touches. They are Kingdom words and Kingdom commands. But, with the velocity of change and challenge in the modern world, how do we live up to this high calling? Impact is Melissa Pratt's answer—grounded in Scripture, inspired by the Spirit, and proven true by the extraordinary pastoral experience and witness that mark her walk with Jesus. Impact is more than a "how to," it is a "why not me and why not here, now?" Read it and change your world.

—Rev. Jim Lyon

General Director, Church of God Ministries

Requests for information should be sent to:

Warner Press, Inc.

PO Box 2499

Anderson, IN 46018-2499

warnerpress.org

Printed in the United States of America.

Editor: Kevin Stiffler

Cover: Curt Corzine

Layout: Katie Miller

ISBN: 978-1-68434-027-9

Impact: That'll Leave a Mark

Melissa Pratt

Table of Contents

This book is dedicated to my Lord and Savior, Jesus Christ, whose eternal word continues to transform my life. It is also dedicated to my incredible husband, Thom, and children, Hannah and Joshua, my daily ministry partners. I also wish to thank the loving people of the Teays Valley Church of God who took a chance on this lady preacher in 2007 and have joined me in tirelessly seeking to impact our community for Christ ever since.

1. Impact:
Colliding with the Culture

Then Jesus came to them and said, "All authority in heaven and on earth has been given to me. Therefore go and make disciples of all nations, baptizing them in the name of the Father and of the Son and of the Holy Spirit, and teaching them to obey everything I have commanded you. And surely I am with you always, to the very end of the age."

—Matthew 2:18–20

I had a car accident, but I didn't realize it until twenty-four hours after it happened. I had gotten on the highway to go to the next exit, headed to the hospital to visit someone. Something broke off of a semi-truck a few hundred feet in front of me. As it came toward me, it hit the lower front of my van with a jolting *boom*. I knew that contact had been made, but I honestly forgot about it by the time I got to the hospital.

The next day I thought, "You know, I probably ought to look at the front of my van to see if there is a scratch or anything on it." *Scratch?!* My entire front bumper had cracked, and whatever hit me went up under the van and did damage there, too—several thousand dollars' worth. In fact, when I took the van to the collision center, they told me it wasn't even in drivable condition, even though I had been driving it for a full day by that time.

Impacts leave a lasting mark. The impact from the truck debris was a negative one. It rearranged my whole front end. I couldn't ignore the impact. I had to deal with it and respond to it. I couldn't take it or leave it. I couldn't pretend it hadn't happened. Changes had to be made to my vehicle as a result of the impact.

As Christians, we should want to impact people with the love of Jesus Christ, as portrayed in the Gospels, in such a way that they cannot just take or leave him—that they can't just ignore him. We should seek to impact others in such a way that they will be forced to consider the impact of Jesus Christ and be altered by it.

Christians need to collide with our culture. We should want to leave a lasting mark on people's lives. We should desire to alter people's circumstances. We should have a passion to engage unbelievers in a way that will change their ideas about God and his people. We should long to have an effect that makes a permanent, positive dent in people's lives. Isn't that the ministry of Jesus?

A Thanksgiving Day editorial in the newspaper told of a school-teacher who asked her first-graders to draw a picture of something for which they were thankful. She thought of how little these children from poor neighborhoods actually had. She figured most of them would draw pictures of turkeys on tables of food. But the teacher was taken aback by the picture Douglas turned in: a simple, childishly drawn hand.

The other students were captivated by the abstract image. Whose hand was it? "I think it must be the hand of God that brings us food," said one. "A farmer, because he grows the turkeys," said another. Finally, when the other students were back at work, the teacher bent over Douglas's desk and asked whose hand it was. "It's your hand," he mumbled.

The teacher recalled that at recess she often took Douglas—a scruffy, deserted child—by the hand. She did that with all the children, but it meant so much to Douglas. Out of all the things for which he could have given thanks, he was most grateful for his teacher's hand.

It was the teacher's personal touch that made a profound impact on that little first-grade boy. People today need a hand that reaches out to them with the love of Christ.

Proper Perspective

Too many Christians have adopted the attitude that we are fighting a losing battle. But the last time I checked, Jesus had already won the war! Yes, it has gotten tougher to live a Christian life. But we cannot abdicate our ability and responsibility to be culture shapers and game changers. Our current North American culture agrees that it is okay for me to be a Christian, as long as my life doesn't impact anyone else's. If we listen to and follow the cultural cues around us, who becomes the "impactor" and who becomes the "impactee"?

Too many Christians have been boxed in and "put in their place." They have resigned from the opportunity to make an impact. But why are we taking our orders from the culture instead of Jesus? Why are we willing to sit in the corner when we are to intentionally be out in the streets impacting others for Christ?

Jesus isn't outdated, and we are not without hope. We can see sweeping transformation in our culture today. After all, Christianity is the greatest game changer of society and culture ever. Christianity has had more impact on history than any other religion or enterprise. Time is measured by the birth of Christ, the years designated as BC or AD.

The idea of human rights and equality comes not from the edict of an earthly ruler or the will of the people, but straight out of the Bible. Christianity has freed women from being the property of a husband to being equals created in the image of God.

Christianity has upheld that children are a gift from God and should be treated as precious. In ancient Greece, infanticide was not only legal, but it was laudable. It was the early Christians who ended the killing of babies. Even today, right now, the pro-life movement is largely Christian. A Christian document called the *Didache*, which dates from the late first century, spoke specifically against abortion. The earliest Christians were pro-life game-changers in their culture.

Sadly, some Christians did own slaves, as the Bible was distorted to support slavery for a time. But ultimately, many of the activists who worked to eradicate slavery were Christians. William Wilberforce, an English politician and believer in Christ, is credited by many historians as the primary force in helping to end the international slave trade. Two-thirds of the members of the American Abolition Society in 1835 were Christian ministers.

It has been documented that after the death and resurrection of Christ, organized charity in his name became prolific. Jesus himself emphasized helping the poor. The Parable of the Good Samaritan is still a classic part of our language today. The Mother Teresas, the Salvation Armies, the religious hospitals, and the church soup kitchens and thrift shops of this world speak every day of the commitment of Jesus to raise the standard of living for the poor. Even the generous character of Santa Claus can be traced back to the spirit of the Christ-child.

The idea of education for the masses and the promotion of literacy had its roots in the Protestant Reformation as the Bible was translated into many languages by Christians. It was the Puritans who enacted the first law that all should be educated—a law called "The Old Deluder Satan Act." The Puritans believed Satan could get a foothold in people's lives because of their ignorance of the Bible—and boy, were they right. Therefore, part of compulsory education was training in the Scriptures, with literacy in general a huge priority.

All but one of the first 123 colleges in colonial America were Christian institutions. While those schools have moved away from their roots, Christianity was their foundation. Even Harvard was founded on this statement: "Let every student be plainly instructed, and earnestly pressed to consider well, the maine end of his life and studies is, to know God and Jesus Christ which is eternal life (John 17:3)."[1]

In the United States, our laws and our system of checks and balances were all rolled out of the principles of Scripture. The vast majority of signers of the U.S. Constitution were Christians. Even science has its roots in Christianity. Almost all the founders of modern science, including Kepler, Boyle, Pascal, Pasteur, and Newton, were Christians who believed God created an orderly universe that could be studied and understood.

I could go on to detail how Christianity has influenced art, music, literature, and architecture. The impact of Christianity on history and culture is simply undeniable. At times, it was a movement of people. At times, great change was ushered in by the courage of one or a few. History also shows us that where there was no stronghold of Christianity in a society, the atrocities in those places were magnified many times over. Think of what took place under the regimes of Hitler, Mao, Stalin, and Pol Pot—all confessed atheists. Well over 100 million murders resulted from these leaders who had no faith in God.[2]

The Example of Christ
And he took the children in his arms, placed his hands on them and blessed them. —Mark 10:16

What a direct impact Jesus made on the children as he reached out to them! There was an embrace that he made possible. He made the move toward them. He drew them close, taking them into his arms, and then he blessed them. They left his presence changed. Jesus blessed them so that hope could grow in their hearts and lives. He blessed them in order to heal and help them. He blessed them

---

1 "Harvard GSAS Christian Community: Shield and 'Veritas' History," accessed March 2, 2017, http://www.hcs.harvard.edu/~gsascf/shield-and-veritas-history/.

2 Adapted from "Faith Facts: The Impact of Christianity," accessed March 2, 2017, http://www.faithfacts.org/christ-and-the-culture/the-impact-of-christianity.

to encourage them and instill confidence in them. He did this so they could dream dreams and become difference-makers themselves. Oh, the impact of the reach of God through Jesus Christ!

Don't we want our churches to be known for more than good preaching and inspiring worship? Don't we want to be viewed as game-changers, as life-changers in our communities? How do we measure our true impact? How many people have we reached out to in an effort to restore them and release them to become full disciples of Jesus and live the best life possible? How many lives have been truly transformed through our ministries? A good reputation is wonderful, but it is time to focus on reclamation instead of reputation. It is time to take back what the Devil has stolen and is stealing from people. It is time to bring the gospel into people's lives in a way that they are forever changed. It is time to rearrange people's ideas about God and the church by making the kind of intentional impact Jesus did.

Allow me to give you an example of the kind of impact I believe we are called to make. The Church of God (Anderson, Indiana) has a shelter for children in Cuttack, India, that our local congregation has supported. The Shelter was started over one hundred years ago to rescue children out of poverty and keep them from being sold into the sex trade as slaves. Ratani Mallick was raised at The Shelter. She was taken there in 1995 when her father died of tuberculosis and her mother was unable to care for her. She was just six years old.

Ratani was nurtured, fed, educated, and cared for. Today, she has earned her master's degree in social work and is seeking employment in that field. She serves at The Shelter now, sharing the help and hope she received with a new generation of children who need to know a bright future is possible. Ratani was rescued. She was restored. And now, she has been released into ministry to do the work of Jesus.

We aren't here to have just a small impact, or even a community or state impact. Rather, Jesus commissioned his disciples, and all who follow him, to have an impact on the world. Beyond sending resources to other nations, it would be impossible for every person to go into every part of the world, right? So, what did Jesus mean? What is our role?

I believe Jesus wants us to live our lives in such a way that we have a maximum impact on those around us. Are our educational facilities safer, more peaceful, and more filled with truth because we work and go to school there? Are the businesses where we earn a living more reputable because we work there? Are our neighborhoods places of mutual support and encouragement because we live there? Are our churches having a maximum impact on the world?

Salt and Light

"You are the salt of the earth. But if the salt loses its saltiness, how can it be made salty again? It is no longer good for anything, except to be thrown out and trampled underfoot.

"You are the light of the world. A town built on a hill cannot be hidden. Neither do people light a lamp and put it under a bowl. Instead they put it on its stand, and it gives light to everyone in the house. In the same way, let your light shine before others, that they may see your good deeds and glorify your Father in heaven." —Matthew 5:13–16

Jesus compared Christians to salt and light. Salt impacts the food it comes into contact with, and light impacts the darkness. Both have transforming powers. Light doesn't just make the darkness better; it transforms it. Salt doesn't just make food better; it transforms or changes the taste. It is noticeable when a light is turned on in a dark room, and it is noticeable when salt is applied to food that has none. Our impact on this world is also supposed to be noticeable. Light points the way so that people can follow a certain path. How effective is your life to guide people to the path of life through Jesus Christ?

Salt is a preservative. It keeps food from rotting. Just as light and darkness are opposites, salt and rotting food could be said to be opposites. Jesus used these metaphors on purpose because of their stark contrasts. Christians aren't supposed to blend in. We aren't to be inconspicuous; we should stand out. People should be able to point to me and say, "She is a Christian" because of the way I am salt and light.

The point of many of the Old Testament laws wasn't to make the Israelites' lives hard or miserable. Instead they were to highlight the fact that God's people are to live dramatically different from the rest of the world. They weren't to live like the Egyptians who had held them captive. They weren't to live like the Canaanites who inhabited the Promised Land before them.

This theme of God's people being different is reiterated in the New Testament in multiple places, but let me share where God spells it out very clearly. It is in Matthew 6:8, right after the chapter on being salt and light. In verse 7, Jesus had just referenced pagans—people who did not follow God. Then, in verse 8, he said, "Do not be like them." The emphasis wasn't so much on what the pagan people were like, but on how we are to be different in an effort to make an impact on those around us.

Christian, do you want to be a game-changer? It won't matter one bit what happens in our churches every Sunday during our "holy huddle" if the plays being called aren't being played out on the field. Some spiritual collisions need to be taking place out in the world.

One such collision was shared with me that made my heart thrill. Someone in our congregation made a decision to leave a lifestyle that didn't glorify God or edify herself. Part of this person's bold decision was the result of the impact our church made on her life.

She shared with me that she felt accepted just as she was when she came to our church, even though she wasn't at a place in life where God wanted her to be (and she knew it). This person confessed that she had tried to make changes before but didn't have the support needed to do so. As this individual made the decision to leave a pattern of sin behind, she felt that she had the support of a church family to help her break free. Acceptance (love) and the challenge and support to change—that is *impact!* Glory to God!

What would happen if we consciously looked for ways to make life-changing impacts in others' lives every day? How can you make an impact...

- ...in your home and in your extended family?
- ...in your school or place of business?
- ...in your neighborhood?
- ...on your friends?
- ...on strangers?

More specifically, what if...

- ...because of our efforts, a homeless person could gain housing?
- ...a scared, pregnant teen chose life, and a believer paid for whatever the needs were during the pregnancy and beyond?
- ...an illiterate person was taught to read?
- ...someone was helped to study for and attain his GED?
- ...we were able to come alongside a family who was about to lose their home and assist them in keeping it?
- ...we were able to mentor a troubled teen and encourage him to stay in school?
- ...a young girl was rescued out of prostitution?

- ...someone who was considering suicide was befriended and prayed for?

- ...we made a life-or-death difference for someone?

- ...we saw people not just connect with us through church, but saw them transformed from lives of addiction and other sinful bondages?

What if?

Going forward, how can we change history? How can we prove that knowing and following Jesus is the best way, the most powerful and peaceful way, to live?

While the tide of culture would suggest that we should just stand back, stay put, and keep our distance, I pray that we will run into others on purpose, with the intent of seeing those around us be rescued, restored, and released to be God's people.

2. A Collective Impact:
The Mark of the Church

They devoted themselves to the apostles' teaching and to fellowship, to the breaking of bread and to prayer. Everyone was filled with awe at the many wonders and signs performed by the apostles. All the believers were together and had everything in common. They sold property and possessions to give to anyone who had need. Every day they continued to meet together in the temple courts. They broke bread in their homes and ate together with glad and sincere hearts, praising God and enjoying the favor of all the people. And the Lord added to their number daily those who were being saved. —Acts 2:42–47

In the animated movie *Ice Age*, a wooly mammoth named Manny, a sloth name Sid, and a tiger named Diego unite on a common mission to return a lost baby to his father. At one point Sid reflects on the unlikely partnership of this trio and says, "We are the weirdest herd I've ever seen."

What a great description of the church! We truly are one strange herd. We are an unlikely group of people with various skills, interests, and talents. Our backgrounds are as diverse as our hairstyles and opinions. We have come together not because of our similarities but because of the salvation we have found in Jesus Christ. It is his transforming power that has united us in life and ministry. It is his mission that has called us into fellowship with one another in order to use our collective influence to make an impact on our culture for the kingdom of God.

There is no better illustration of a Christ-community having a collective impact than the first-century church. Acts 2:42–47 details the way the early believers made a fast-growing and lasting mark on those around them.

A Collected Community

The church is a massive group of individuals who have been collected or gathered by God through the blood of Jesus into this herd, into this pack, called the family of God or, as the Scriptures put it, the "body of Christ." We're not included because we all follow the same pop stars or sports figures. We aren't included because we all enjoy the same television shows and movies, nor are we members because we share the same hobbies or are all best friends outside of church.

We are included because God has instituted the church, the body of Christ, to represent Jesus on earth. We belong because he has made it possible for us to relate to one another, as a spiritual community, in a way that wouldn't be possible apart from the blood of Jesus Christ.

There is one body and one Spirit, just as you were called to one hope when you were called; one Lord, one faith, one baptism; one God and Father of all. —Ephesians 4:4–6a

Only those who are believers in Christ, whose sins have been forgiven through his blood, are members of this body. The strategy of this collected community is that, as we go out into all the earth, we represent Christ everywhere we go by impacting those in our circles of influence. We not only have the name "body of Christ," but we also have a very distinct mission. We are to be Christ on earth. Have you ever considered the magnitude of that assignment? You and I are called to be Jesus Christ on earth. It is an immense calling and responsibility.

The first-century church took this calling seriously. They knew that in order to become what Christ intended them to be, they had to spend time with one another. They were eager to get together to study God's Word. They were anxious to celebrate Communion together. They longed to see one another and to gather for fellowship. They couldn't wait to hear the stories of impact that were constantly taking place. Yes, they had their individual lives, but they had a life together that was fulfilling, compelling, and energizing. Missing church gatherings wasn't something they entertained. They knew that they were better together. They knew that they had a greater impact collectively. It wasn't a struggle to get them to assemble; they were glad to come together. It was their commitment to assemble and spend time together in worship and the Word that led to the shaping of their identity as Christ's body on earth. God knit them together so he could use them to make an impact.

A Collaborative Community

We may not all have the same interests, but we are all to have the same goal when it comes to representing Christ on earth. I love the "all-in" feeling I get when I read the Acts 2 passage. *Everyone* was filled with awe. There were miracles and signs and wonders taking place in their worship services. The body of Christ was a conduit for the supernatural. What Jesus had done on earth was being experienced and multiplied through his body. All the believers were together and were engaged in what God was doing in and through them. They had everything in common. They loved hanging out and doing life and ministry together. The energy in those gatherings must have been explosive! Imagine a church service where everyone was "all in" to what was going on. And imagine the explosive impact when that energy would spill out into the streets and impact those on the outside.

The coming together wasn't the only collaborative part. They were doing more than collaborating in worship. Outside of those times, they were conspiring to convey the gospel message through acts of service in their community. They were taking Jesus to the world! They sold stuff in order to fund their mission. They haggled with the owners of the "Palestine Pawn Shop" just so they could get the best deals on their goods in order to give the money to people who had needs. Jesus hadn't told them to sell stuff to help people out; it was just a natural overflow from their collectedness. That collectedness led to collaboration and started pouring out in practical ministry on the streets.

Notice it doesn't say that twenty percent of the people did eighty percent of the work, and only five percent of the people tithed. The early church had a much more collaborative view of life than most Christians do today. They shared with one another freely. How cool would it be for the church to have a reputation in the community as being a place full of "excessive sharers"?

Every believer has something to bring to the table. You have gifts and skills and interests and connections and ideas and resources that can be used in concert with someone else's. And when we put it all together under the leadership of the Holy Spirit, then *boom—* we create an impact for the kingdom of God.

A Caring Community

A few years ago, someone in our town asked me if I was the leader of the "Hospital on the Hill." When I asked him to clarify his question, he told me our church had earned that nickname. That was thrilling for me to hear, because that's how a Christ-community ought to be known. Jesus never said, "I am too tired to care." He never said, "I don't have the money to care." He never said, "It is someone else's responsibility to care." Remember, we are to do the ministry of Jesus on earth. Caring for the hurting people in our communities is paramount, and every person matters, no matter what.

The early believers gave to *anyone* who had a need. They didn't discriminate. They didn't qualify who would receive help. Murderers, thieves, adulterers, liars, drunks, hookers, and hoodlums were all welcome. The rich and the poor were equally received. The young and the old were greeted with open arms, and all kinds of people from all kinds of backgrounds joined the Jesus movement. Why? *Because caring people make it safe to belong.*

When churches become safe places and people know that no matter what they have done or where they have been that they will be welcomed, cared for, respected, and loved, they will lay down their pasts and their pride to find out more. Caring communities don't get fixated on where people are, but on where God wants to take them.

Do we still believe God has a "hope and a future" (Jeremiah 29:11) for people regardless of their present status? My heartbeat is that no one in our church would ever be condemned or shamed for being honest about the reality of his or her personal story, but that we would embrace and support everyone as they walk into a victorious future.

It was absolutely beautiful one Wednesday night to witness the spontaneous testimony of one of our members who shared about her struggle with addiction. As the story flowed from her lips, compassion flowed from the congregation, and, as this woman took her seat, many people went over to embrace her. It was a moment of impact I'll never forget. That is the kind of care with which we are to treat one another. That is the kind of genuine compassion that leaves a God-print on a broken heart and broken life.

Romans 12:15 says we are to "mourn with those who mourn." When people are hurting and grieving, it should stir us and move us to action. God wants to use every believer to help someone else make it through the day with courage and encouragement. Caring leaves a lasting impression and is attractive to those who are searching for the truth.

Ask about the arthritis or chemotherapy. Ask what it is like now that someone has become a stay-at-home mom. Ask how the job change or the move to a new community has gone. Ask for follow-up information after people share prayer requests. Ask what it is like now that the kids are grown and have left the nest. Ask how the ballgame, recital, or test went. Ask how someone is managing while caring for an aging parent. Ask how someone is coping three months, six months, and years after they have lost a loved one. Caring communities remind people that they are not forgotten.

Remembering and reaching out to those who are hurting creates a life-changing and healing impact.

A Corrective Community

This whole "all-in" collaborative and caring spirit that was exhibited in the first-century church was so much the norm that, when Ananias and Sapphira lied to the apostles, they were called out on it (Acts 5:1–11). Accountability was super important in the early church. If someone stepped out of line, one of the brothers or sisters stepped into that person's way. Hypocrisy wasn't tolerated—period.

It would be irresponsible and sinful for pastors to tell their parishioners that God loves them so much that however they choose to live is fine with God. That is not the case. In fact, God has established principles for the discipline of his people through his body to help people see their need for confession, repentance, restitution, and reconciliation. Scripture passages about discipline remind us that unbelievers aren't the only people who need to be impacted from time to time.

Discipline involves training. Pastors and leaders need to be responsible to teach what God expects of his people. Discipline also involves encouragement and support to ward off sinful choices. We are all accountable to and for one another; we all need to be invested in one another's spiritual success. When we see someone headed off course, we need to prayerfully and lovingly find a way to speak the truth (Ephesians 4:15). We need to personally develop an attitude that welcomes discipline and loving correction, because it could save us from destructive mistakes. Consider this advice:

Whoever loves discipline loves knowledge, but whoever hates correction is stupid. —Proverbs 12:1

Yes, it actually uses the word *stupid*!

The goals of discipline should include the following:

- To keep a person from being lost to Satan.
- To prevent hurt and misunderstandings.
- To protect the unity of the church.
- To keep families from falling apart.
- To keep us from accepting false teachings (see Acts 20:28–31).
- To keep someone's personal witness from being compromised.
- To keep the witness of the entire body of Christ intact.

Guess what? One hypocrite, in the world's estimation, makes hypocrites of us all. Correction is critical; we want to make the right kind of impact on this watching world.

It is not okay to purposely hurt people, and it is not okay to not feel remorse when we do hurt people. It is not okay to be unrepentant and to refuse reconciliation. The reason we can't just live any way we please is because we represent Christ on earth.

Jesus lived to please the Father; he lived to demonstrate holiness. I firmly believe that no one has ever achieved the character of holiness without discipline. I'm not talking about beating people up with Bible verses and harsh words, or about judgment, shame, and excommunication. I am talking about speaking the truth in love so that our lives can have optimal impact.

A Celebratory Community

Acts 2:47 says the people were praising God and enjoying the favor of the community. They were winning at home! They were high-fiving God and one another. They were exchanging their God-stories. When one person won, they all won. They were happy for one another, and there was no spirit of competition. People were being saved and filled with the Spirit of God. The church was making an impact because they were willing to associate with one another (collected), to work together (collaborative), to look beyond their own needs to the needs of others (caring), and to be accountable one to another (corrective). They had many reasons to celebrate.

Romans 12:15 tells us that when others rejoice, we should rejoice with them. This is a spiritual command. One reason I love social media is because when I read about how someone succeeds in some way—whether in sports or career or academics or whatever—I thoroughly enjoy congratulating that person. It is fun to celebrate a victory no matter who is holding the title.

Appropriate celebration gives God glory and bolsters the church's sense of connectedness and collaboration. I believe the act of celebrating something wholesome or victorious is a spiritual expression that builds up the body of Christ and is attractive to those who are looking for a reason to celebrate. It makes a wonderful impact. A win for you is a win for me, and it becomes a win for God's kingdom when it makes an impact for Christ.

———

How committed are you to being Christ on earth? Have you dedicated yourself to being a part of the collaborative effort of the church? Are you involved in caring for the needs represented in your congregation and your community? Are you open to correction and looking out for those who might be straying? Are you jealous of the victories in other people's lives, or are you adding to their celebration by celebrating with them?

I believe every one of these Christ-community characteristics is appealing to people on the outside looking in. How "New Testament" can we get? How much can we look like the first-century church? How much can you and I look like Jesus here on earth as we live out his life in a Christ-community? How can we come even closer together to make a collective impact?

3. A Gospel Impact:
Living the Transformed Life

The Spirit of the Sovereign LORD is on me,
  because the LORD has anointed me
  to proclaim good news to the poor.
He has sent me to bind up the brokenhearted,
  to proclaim freedom for the captives
  and release from darkness for the prisoners,
to proclaim the year of the LORD's favor
  and the day of vengeance of our God,
to comfort all who mourn,
  and provide for those who grieve in Zion—
to bestow on them a crown of beauty
  instead of ashes,
the oil of joy
  instead of mourning,
and a garment of praise
  instead of a spirit of despair.
They will be called oaks of righteousness,
  a planting of the LORD
  for the display of his splendor. —Isaiah 61:1–3

The prophet Isaiah foretold the job description of Jesus, the Messiah, hundreds of years before Jesus' birth. To help people make the connection that Jesus was the Messiah, Jesus picked up a copy of that job description from Isaiah 61 and read it out loud in the synagogue (Luke 4:18–19). In that moment, he was introducing people to the impact he had come to make on who they were and how they experienced life.

Through his proclamation, Jesus was setting the stage for inviting people to follow him—not only into believing something and knowing something but also into a way of *living* something they had not yet known. It is one thing to "know" the gospel but an entirely different thing to be impacted by the gospel and live out its message. Both involve a choice. Both involve faith. One is foundational to the next. You have to know and believe something before you can live it, but oftentimes people who know and believe aren't impacted by that information to go on and live out their "knowing."

Living Happy

Just what is this gospel way of living about? What impact is the gospel message supposed to have on Christ followers? First, to be impacted by the gospel is to live happy.

Isaiah 61:1 tells us that part of the "Jesus way" of life includes receiving good news. Good news is happy news. I remember how I felt when I found out I was expecting our first child. I couldn't wait to share the good news. I called someone at 2:00 AM and woke her up to tell her! I couldn't help myself. Even though I was packing on the pounds, I walked around like I was floating on air. That good news brought Thom and me great happiness. I was carrying something inside of my body that I knew would impact my life in a positive way at the end of those nine months. What was happening inside of me would change my life for the good forever.

The good news of a child coming into our home gave us a new focus. We spent a lot of time reading about all things baby. That focus took us through real transformation. We became parents before we ever held our little girl. We rearranged things in our house to accommodate another person. Our little princess was the topic of lots of conversations between the two of us and with other people. There was an element of excitement that was constant. Even though I had a high-risk pregnancy that wasn't easy, and even though I got huger than huge and could hardly walk by the end, I experienced happiness and joy the entire nine months. I anticipated the "good news" I was carrying becoming something even better when I gave birth. Good news turned into great love and joy the moment I got to see my sweet daughter's face.

What I'm trying to portray with this illustration is that even though life itself can be difficult, if we accept the good news of the gospel, there is a quality of happiness, contentment, and anticipation that sustains us through the challenging times—even when those times last beyond nine months. The gospel message is happy news that we receive into our being, and it impacts our outside, everyday life.

The poor are recipients of the good news Jesus came to give (Isaiah 61:1). These are not necessarily those who are financially impoverished. The poor are any people who could use some good news and a change in their circumstances.

People who understand that we are all spiritually impoverished without God are those who welcome the good news of the gospel into their hearts. When people say Jesus changed their lives for the better, they are saying that a blessedness, a happiness deeper than the world's definition of happy, has become their anchor. Here is the essence of this good news: Something happened over two thousand years ago, and the reality and power of that event can be experienced in your heart and life today—and every day of your life. What an impact!

The good news is more than salvation and freedom from sin. It is the reality that we can know God and we never have to be alone. Once someone accepts Christ, he comes to live on the inside of that person forever in a way that perpetuates this good news.

Because Christ lives in me, I never have to panic. Because Christ lives in me, I am never without hope. Because Christ lives in me, I have access to unlimited power and resources. Because Christ lives in me, I can have courage. Because Christ lives in me, one day I will be out of here and headed into a perfect, eternal scenario that is better than my best day here.

If you want to live out the gospel so that you make an impact on a skeptical world, show them the difference it makes to have Jesus on the inside of your life. Rather than being led by our emotion, allowing our circumstances to dictate how we respond to people and events, let's allow what has happened inside of us to help us respond in faith, confidence, and contentment.

Living Whole

To be impacted by the gospel is also to live whole. Isaiah 61:1 includes this in Jesus' job description: "He has sent me to bind up the brokenhearted." I didn't experience brokenheartedness until I was forty years old. Up to that point, my life had been fairly easy and comfortable. But in my early forties, a series of disappointments left me bruised and battered on the inside. The core of my identity was not only shaken but shattered. What I learned through the experience of healing was something I had known in my head, but had never experienced in my heart. It was good news with a healing impact. Here it is: *People will fail us, but God never will. And when people do fail us, God is more than enough to sustain and heal us.*

Too often, we get hurt and stay hurt. We ruminate on the hurt. We rehearse the hurt over and over in our minds. Sometimes we share the hurt with others to feel validated that we have a right to feel hurt. You know the old saying, "Misery loves company." We allow the hurt to build unhealthy walls in our lives that cut us off from people. We allow the hurt to redefine our future, hold us back, and diminish us. We allow the hurt to make us angry and bitter in our hearts. This ultimately has negative impacts on our physical health, our sleep, our job performance, our relationships, and our quality of life.

Brokenhearted people, if they stay brokenhearted, will live broken lives. However, as we are impacted by the gospel, God brings healing to our splintered hearts to help us live full, whole lives. He wants to strengthen us. We are the ones the Bible calls "overcomers." We are the ones who can have victory in our lives.

"The Lord does not look at the things people look at. People look at the outward appearance, but the Lord looks at the heart."
—1 Samuel 16:7b

God looks at the condition of our hearts when it comes to dealing with sin in our lives. He looks at the condition of our hearts when it comes to our sincerity in our walk with him. He looks at the condition of our hearts when it comes to our dependence upon him and whether or not we should be put in certain positions. But God isn't just interested in your heart for salvation purposes or for leadership possibilities. God is interested in your heart because what breaks your heart breaks his.

When you hurt, God hurts with you. Like a parent who enters into the pain her or his child feels due to disappointment, rejection, or betrayal, God is in tune with our suffering and pain. It moves him. As parents, we wish we could do something to make things better when our children are brokenhearted, but we serve a God who *can* do something when his children are brokenhearted. He can bring healing and transformation that causes us to become better and stronger because of what we have endured—better and stronger than we would have been had we never had a broken heart in the first place. That which Satan would use to destroy us, God uses for our benefit as he draws close to heal us (Romans 8:28). And when unbelievers catch a glimpse of God's healing power in our lives, it leaves a lasting impression on them that compels them to draw closer. What a beautiful impact of the gospel!

When God heals our broken hearts, he gives us the capacity to see things from a different perspective. Even when we have been unjustly and horrifically wronged, he shows us how we can frame what has happened to us in such a way that can help us move forward, not stay stuck in a place of despair. He gives us an eternal perspective. He shows us how what we have been through can become a tool for us to help others. He takes us from pained to purposeful through his healing mercies. As we desire his healing and surrender to that healing, he will bring people into our lives who minister to us in personal and practical ways. The healing power of Christ comes often through his people, his body, as we come alongside one another in times of difficulty.

Perhaps it is when we are brokenhearted that we have the ability to see Jesus the most clearly. Luke 24 tells us about two disciples who were headed to Emmaus following Jesus' crucifixion. They were heartbroken. But then Jesus joined them on their walk. They hadn't already thought to invite him to journey with them; perhaps they didn't know that they could or should. They really didn't expect him to be available since, after all, he had been crucified. So they didn't look for him to offer any insight into their experience of brokenness.

Sometimes we don't think to ask for Jesus to show up when we are brokenhearted. Our pain clouds our minds, and we struggle with finding what we feel might be the right way to deal with things. But Jesus is good at inviting himself into our suffering.

After they talked with Jesus a while, it was in the breaking of bread that these two disciples clearly saw Jesus for who he was, the resurrected Christ—and that changed everything. Through broken bread, broken people saw Jesus as he entered into their broken story.

Perhaps you are brokenhearted. Maybe you don't see any silver lining in the clouds. Maybe you feel like damaged goods, like someone no one would want to hang with. Jesus is stepping into your path. He is drawing close. Open the eyes of your heart to see him. He has healing words to share and healing people to share with you to offer his support. They will impact your now and give you hope for tomorrow.

To be impacted by the gospel is to live whole. Give your broken heart to Jesus so he can do a wonderful, healing work in your life.

Living Free

To be impacted by the gospel is also to live free. The last part of Isaiah 61:1 details this aspect of the Messiah's job description: "to proclaim freedom for the captives and release from darkness for the prisoners." Freedom.

"If the Son sets you free you will be free indeed." —John 8:36

We can live free in every way. God can free our hearts from sin. He can free our minds from self-destructive and anxious thoughts. He can free our bodies from compulsive and addictive behaviors. He can free us from the approval of other people. The gospel has a chain-breaking, liberating impact on our lives.

Living out the gospel means that we live and walk in true freedom.

It is for freedom that Christ has set us free. —Galatians 5:1a

God doesn't want you to be oppressed, controlled, or mastered by anything that will limit you or steal life from you. The way to enjoy this kind of freedom is to be submitted to God and his purposes. He has the power to break every chain in your life. Everything you wish you could stop doing, he has the power to enable you to stop doing. Everything you wish you could start doing, he has the power to motivate you to begin.

I will walk about in freedom,
for I have sought out your precepts. —Psalm 119:45

What are God's precepts? They are his way of doing life. You see, when we live by God's standards, we maintain our freedom. *But wait a minute, doesn't the fact that God has rules mean that our freedom is restricted?* Not at all! God's rules are the rules that enable us to live as free as possible. Satan's strategy and the rules that come with a sinful lifestyle bind us and take away the freedom we were created to enjoy in Christ.

You, my brothers and sisters, were called to be free. —Galatians 5:13a

There is now no condemnation for those who are in Christ Jesus, because through Christ Jesus the law of the Spirit who gives life has set you free from the law of sin and death. —Romans 8:1–2

If you are in Christ, you are *not* what has happened to you, and you are not what you have done to cope with what has happened to you. You can be free from your past and free from what you have become.

What a life-altering impact the gospel has! God, in Christ, has come to give you freedom to become like Jesus. He has come to free you from oppressive and heavy emotions, to free you from condemnation, shame, and judgment. He has come to free you from addictions that will destroy your finances, your friendships, and your future. Get free and stay free by following God's precepts rather than chasing worldly experiences that lead back into bondage.

In many ways, we are a lot like the people of Jeremiah's time. Here are the charges God leveled against them:

"My people have committed two sins:
They have forsaken me,
the spring of living water,
and have dug their own cisterns,
broken cisterns that cannot hold water." —Jeremiah 2:13

When you try to get what you need for life from that which is broken, it will lead you to compromise your freedom. It will send you to fake wells and broken cisterns, into all kinds of experiences and relationships that are full of empty promises, deception, and entrapment—right into the grip of Satan and sin. But you were made for more. You were made for freedom, the freedom to love and know and serve God.

Living Strong

Finally, to be impacted by the gospel is to live strong. The end of Isaiah 61:3 says that we can be firm and unmoving in our faith:

They will be called oaks of righteousness,
a planting of the LORD
for the display of his splendor.

For those who follow Christ, perhaps the best compliment to us would be, "Nice roots." We are to be strong, permanent, fixed in our faith, and unbending to the ways of the world. We are to be established as believers, not wishy-washy individuals who are "Jesus people" on Sunday but live some other way on Monday. We are to stand tall and stand out for the display of God's splendor.

But notice what Isaiah says after this:

They will rebuild the ancient ruins
and restore the places long devastated;
they will renew the ruined cities
that have been devastated for generations. —Isaiah 61:4

What does it mean that they (we) will rebuild ancient ruins and restore devastated places and renew ruined cities? As we are "oaks of righteousness," as we live strong, as we are uncompromising in our beliefs, we will be a witness that is compelling to unbelievers. We will play a role in transforming the communities around us. We will serve and help in places that need restoration. We will be a part of renewal in our culture during our very lifetimes. This is impact. God will display his splendor through his people who live strong lives.

We live in a time when the foundation of Christian faith in North America has been destroyed. This generation is being born into a spiritual wasteland. What once was valued and shared now lies in ruins. God is looking for some people who will choose to live out the impact of the gospel, who will choose to be like trees planted by streams of living water, who will yield fruit in season, who won't be moved by every wind and wave of doctrine and drama that comes along. Grow strong. Stand strong. Live strong so that others will come to know the same happy, whole, and free life you have come to enjoy in Christ.

To be impacted by the gospel means to let Jesus fulfill his job description in you. Jesus Christ, through the power of the Holy Spirit, wants to bring happiness, wholeness, freedom, and strength to your life so that his splendor will be seen in the world today.

4. Words of Impact:
The Power of Your Story

Then, leaving her water jar, the woman went back to the town and said to the people, "Come, see a man who told me everything I ever did. Could this be the Messiah?" They came out of the town and made their way toward him. —John 4:28–30

Many of the Samaritans from that town believed in him because of the woman's testimony, "He told me everything I ever did." So when the Samaritans came to him, they urged him to stay with them, and he stayed two days. And because of his words many more became believers.

They said to the woman, "We no longer believe just because of what you said; now we have heard for ourselves, and we know that this man really is the Savior of the world." —John 4:39–42

If someone asked you to describe who you are and what you are about, what pertinent things would you include? Would you talk about who your parents were, where you grew up, what schools you attended, or what you do for a living? Would you list who your siblings or spouse or children are? Would you describe what you like to do for fun or those you know who also live in the area?

If someone asked you about Jesus Christ, what would you say about him? How would you describe him? Would you talk about his birthplace in Bethlehem two thousand years ago? Would you share how he is the central figure not only in Christianity but also in all of history? Would you speak about how he only had a short ministry of three and a half years that didn't even begin until he turned thirty? Perhaps you would quote what he said of himself:

"I am the way and the truth and the life. No one comes to the Father except through me." —John 14:6

Would you recount Jesus' claim to be God in the flesh and talk about how he provided for the salvation of all people through his death, burial, and resurrection? Would you talk about your personal experience with Jesus to help others make a decision for him?

If we are going to impact people for the kingdom of God, we need to be comfortable talking about Jesus Christ. After all, he is the main character in the gospel story.

Accepted

The New Testament has many examples of people sharing the gospel message. Among them was the unnamed woman at the well. When it came to talking about Jesus, she was a compelling communicator. Many people became Christ-followers because of her testimony. If this woman taught a "Witnessing 101" class, what might she reveal about sharing her testimony with a town of people who once reviled her? Perhaps she would begin this way: *"Jesus accepted me as I was."*

Jesus was the only completely holy, sinless person who ever lived. He was a Jewish rabbi, a master teacher of the Scriptures. He took the initiative to engage a Samaritan woman, which in that day was crossing racial and gender lines. Not only that, but he risked coming to and being alone with a woman of great scandal. There was a reason this woman was at the well at the hottest part of the day. She went alone to avoid the whispers and stares of the other women who knew who she was, what she had done, and how she was still living.

I think a lot of people are hindered by their sin when it comes to exploring a life with Jesus. Many people think they have to be perfect or "have their act together" before they can come to Christ. They have a sense that they aren't good enough for God. And it's true; we aren't. Our sin puts distance between us and God. We aren't good enough for God, but hallelujah, he is "God enough" for us! God accepts us where we are in order to have an honest conversation with us about our sin problem. He enables us to acknowledge it, confess it, and, by God's grace, have it forgiven and removed from our lives.

The woman at the well was used to having people scrutinize her life. She was the "talk of the town," but not in a good way. Jesus wanted to talk about her life—not to shun and shame her, but to bring her to a place of healing and redemption. He wanted her to know that her sinful condition wasn't a barrier for him, and that in spite of who she was and what she had done, he still wanted a relationship with her. So Jesus got right into the thick of the woman's story:

He told her, "Go, call your husband and come back."

"I have no husband," she replied.

Jesus said to her, "You are right when you say you have no husband. The fact is, you have had five husbands, and the man you now have is not your husband. What you have just said is quite true."
—John 4:16–18

The fact that this woman went from man to man and was intimate with them was indicative of a bigger problem. Helping her "own" her behavior was the first step in getting her to evaluate the condition of her heart. Jesus wanted her to see her brokenness. For until we admit that we are broken, we can't truly be fixed.

Repenting of sin and choosing a different way of life in Christ starts with getting real about where we are. This woman was obviously searching for something. You don't go from relationship to relationship without a desire or need for something, and superficial relationships and one-night stands won't ever be the solution.

Jesus is the God full of grace *and* truth. His grace allows him to meet us where we are, and his truth enables us to move from where we are to where he is.

Jesus accepts us where we are in order to help us face that which is destroying our lives. Why? Because he wants us to really live. While the people of this woman's town sought to destroy her with their words because of her sin, Jesus sought to help her overcome her sin by first accepting her where she was. People need to hear there is nothing they have done or could ever do that would cause God to stop his pursuit of them. Nothing is hidden from him, and nothing anyone does could change his desire for a relationship with that person. As you seek to make an impact by telling your story, be sure to include that Jesus takes people right where they are so that they can go be with him where he is.

Things I Didn't Know

The second part of the woman's "Witnessing 101" sharing may have included a statement such as this: *"Jesus taught me things I didn't know."*

People today often reject Jesus because they don't understand who he is or why he came. We live in a day when biblical illiteracy is common. Sharing our story is critical because many people don't even know how to pursue God. They have lots of bad ideas about religion. The purity of a relationship with God has gotten twisted and perverted to the point where people think being a Christian means you are gullible, uninformed, old-fashioned, or stupid. Believing that God exists and that he loves you makes no sense to them. Knowing God seems so complicated that no one could ever understand it, so why try? We must share our experiences with Jesus because there is a whole generation that needs to "un-learn" what they think it means to be a Christ-follower.

The woman at the well thought she knew some spiritual stuff, but she didn't have things quite straight:

"Sir," the woman said, "I can see that you are a prophet. Our ancestors worshiped on this mountain, but you Jews claim that the place where we must worship is in Jerusalem."

"Woman," Jesus replied, "believe me, a time is coming when you will worship the Father neither on this mountain nor in Jerusalem. You Samaritans worship what you do not know; we worship what we do know, for salvation is from the Jews. Yet a time is coming and has now come when the true worshipers will worship the Father in the Spirit and in truth, for they are the kind of worshipers the Father seeks. God is spirit, and his worshipers must worship in the Spirit and in truth." —John 4:19–24

The woman did recognize Jesus as a prophet. Many people today also give Jesus prophet status. They can't deny the historical record that he lived and that he had a profound impact on the spiritual climate of his day. And because they know he lived a good life, they believe they know who he is and what he was and is about. But there is so much more to learn about Christ and living God's way than any of us have yet experienced. We don't know it all.

A relationship with Jesus is a learning relationship. In Matthew 11:29, he invites us simply to learn from him.

The woman at the well went on to talk about temple worship versus mountain worship, and Jesus started to teach her that it wasn't about a physical place for worship. It was about Spirit and truth, about the condition of a person's heart. Oh, how this world needs to understand that a relationship with Jesus impacts our hearts! That impact begins when Jesus lovingly addresses our sin right where we are (acceptance). He then teaches us truth to enable us to engage him on an entirely different level.

Following Christ is a spiritual learning experience. Part of who we are is spirit, and from that place we engage with God on a daily basis regardless of our physical location. Many people mistakenly think a relationship with God is about a church building or a corporate gathering. In fact, it is really about your own being, your own body, your own person, your own past, present, and future. That is where God seeks to engage with people—on a one-on-one basis.

While the woman at the well had some spiritual knowledge, it wasn't complete. She had some truth mixed with error. Jesus told her in verse 22 that she was worshiping what she didn't even know. He taught her that she needed to look to the Jews, for they had been chosen to be a light to the world. The Messiah was coming from the Jewish people. The woman then revealed that she did know something very important:

"I know that Messiah" (called Christ) "is coming. When he comes, he will explain everything to us." —John 4:25

I wonder if Jesus smiled and winked at her when he told her that he was the Messiah? I am sure her jaw dropped to the ground as she considered the possibility of his claim. There she was, a person with some spiritual knowledge, having a conversation with Jesus himself, but she hadn't recognized him for who he was. Isn't that a commentary on today's culture?

Many people in this world possess spiritual knowledge, but there is an inability to see Jesus for who he is. We have to get after it. We have to teach people the truth about who Jesus is so that they can be led and taught by Jesus himself.

A Great Offer

The third part of the woman's "Witnessing 101" sharing may have been the portion that made such a great impact on the townspeople: *"Jesus offered me more than I could have imagined."*

Look at the first part of the story:

When a Samaritan woman came to draw water, Jesus said to her, "Will you give me a drink?" (His disciples had gone into the town to buy food.)

The Samaritan woman said to him, "You are a Jew and I am a Samaritan woman. How can you ask me for a drink?" (For Jews do not associate with Samaritans.)

Jesus answered her, "If you knew the gift of God and who it is that asks you for a drink, you would have asked him and he would have given you living water."

"Sir," the woman said, "you have nothing to draw with and the well is deep. Where can you get this living water? Are you greater than our father Jacob, who gave us the well and drank from it himself, as did also his sons and his livestock?"

Jesus answered, "Everyone who drinks this water will be thirsty again, but whoever drinks the water I give them will never thirst. Indeed, the water I give them will become in them a spring of water welling up to eternal life."

The woman said to him, "Sir, give me this water so that I won't get thirsty and have to keep coming here to draw water." —John 4:7–15

Jesus moved the topic of conversation from physical water to spiritual water, a concept difficult for the woman to understand. Her mind was on a physical reality, not a spiritual truth. It is also difficult for the world to understand spiritual principles because they are so foreign to our usual way of life. Maybe the woman was thinking, "Living water? This is well water. It is just sitting there. Maybe he means running water like water from a stream or a fountain" (which was actually closer to the spiritual principle Jesus was introducing).

Though the woman didn't understand it totally, her mind was redirected to a spiritual place, and she asked Jesus if he was greater than Jacob. She was speaking of the Jacob who had descended from Abraham and Isaac. (The Samaritans looked to Jacob as their founder.) Jesus went on to explain that he wasn't speaking of well water or a running stream, but a different kind of water—water that would quench thirst eternally. This water had a spiritual property and power that would lead to contentment and eternal life. Wow! What an impact that statement must have made on the woman as she realized that Jesus was offering far more than she could have dreamed.

This offer of living water is the good news part of the gospel that people need to hear. It isn't "too good to be true"! What Jesus offers is the real deal. You can live with peace and contentment in this life, with great joy, and you can also live forever in the paradise called heaven.

The woman at the well was changed by her meeting with Jesus. We know this because she went to the very people she had tried to avoid before. She went to her "enemies" to tell them the good news she had heard. We might expect her to want to keep this offer of living water and eternal life to herself. It doesn't seem like she would want to share it with people who had mistreated her, but that is exactly what she did.

The impact of the gospel, of encountering Jesus, will cause people to love even those who have hated them. It will compel people to leave behind things they thought were important, just as the woman at the well left her water jar behind. It will cause them to ask more and more questions about Jesus in an effort to grow closer to him. As they do, that thirst, that desire in their souls, that thing they have been searching for through relationships or money or affirmation or success, will become satisfied in Christ as they receive from him more than they could have ever dreamed.

At the heart of this woman's testimony—a testimony that turned an entire town upside down—was simply her encounter with Jesus and what it meant to her. Oh, the transforming power of the gospel message when we just tell people what Jesus has done for us! But we have to open up our mouths to declare it.

What could we include in our stories? How about this: *Jesus is the sinless Son of God who made a way for you to be forgiven of your sin. He offers you eternity in heaven. He will accept you where you are, teach you what you need to know, and give you a satisfying life in him that will be beyond anything you can imagine.*

Don't wait to start sharing your own words of impact.

5. A Courageous Impact:
Stepping Up and Out in Faith

The Spirit God gave us does not make us timid, but gives us power, love and self-discipline. —2 Timothy 1:7

When Star Trek appeared on television in the late 1960s, the announcer at the beginning of each episode talked about the spaceship's mission: "to explore strange new worlds, to seek out new life and new civilizations, to boldly go where no one has gone before."

We live in an ever-changing world. The twists and turns of the culture speak this truth about life and ministry: *We have never been here before.* The complexities of diversity and the sensitivities that stretch to countless special interests and individuals are staggering. The different ways of being and doing that have become normal, routine, and expected in the last decade have altered North American culture to the point where it is no longer predictable.

While we are far removed from the cultures of ancient peoples and the first-century church, the need for God's people to be strong and courageous hasn't changed. If anything, it has only intensified, as the call to courage for the church is "to boldly go where no one has gone before." The intricacies of human relationships, the varied opinions on how best to protect individuals and their civil liberties, and the secularization of our schools and workplaces put pressure on the church to "learn its place" in a sea of political correctness. Christian courage is required now perhaps more than ever.

If the church is to be on the march with mission and purpose, it will have to be filled with men and women who have Holy Spirit power to demonstrate godly courage. We need to not only be willing to have the necessary conversations, but we need to be leading them. That which offended God in Bible times still does. That which he offers is still available. And it will take courage to share both messages in our world today. The Scriptures are replete with countless stories of men and women who took a stand for God, who made an impact, and who positively shaped history.

The Courage to Choose Life and Liberation

Jochebed was a woman of the Old Testament who exhibited great courage as she parented and protected her children. Certainly, it takes courage to be a mom or dad. Parenting is a lot of responsibility. It can't happen successfully without courage.

Jochebed must have been a great mom. Her three children all excelled. They all had the foundation they needed to face those forks in the road that life brings to each of us. They successfully navigated through identity issues, questions, and doubts to accomplish what they needed to when the moment called for it. They all were impacted by their mother's courage and faith. Their names were Moses, Aaron, and Miriam.

Moses, of course became one of the greatest leaders ever recorded in history as he negotiated the release of millions of hostages and led that entire group out of captivity toward the Promised Land. His brother, Aaron, became Israel's first high priest, the founder of the Aaronic priesthood. And then there was the gifted worship leader, poetess, and prophetess, their sister, Miriam. Jochebed had a lot to be proud of in her three children, who grew up to lead and shape the culture of an entire nation.

The conditions surrounding the birth of Moses were tough. The Hebrew people were growing fast numerically. The Egyptians were afraid that the Hebrews might overtake them, causing the Egyptians to lose their source of slave labor, so Pharaoh ordered that every male Hebrew baby was to be killed. When Moses was born, Jochebed displayed immense courage by hiding her son from Pharaoh's men. She made a basket out of papyrus and set him afloat on the Nile River. His big sister, Miriam, kept an eye on him from afar.

Pharaoh's daughter went to the river and discovered the floating baby. She was instantly drawn to Moses and decided to take him as her son. Sister Miriam was fast on her feet. She quickly asked the princess if she would like for her to go find a Hebrew woman to nurse the baby for her. The princess thought it was a wonderful idea, and guess who got the job? Moses' own mother, Jochebed. What a special gift from God! When Jochebed had done all she could and baby Moses could no longer be kept quiet, God stepped in to reveal the next phase of Moses' protection. He would be cared for by his mother in the palace.

Choosing to protect Moses' life meant that Jochebed risked her own as she defied Pharaoh's edict. How different would the Israelites' story be today without Moses? The courage of one mom led to the liberation of millions of people just a few decades later. We never know how one life will impact the world. William Wilberforce, Harriet Tubman, Clara Barton, John Wesley, Martin Luther King, Jr., Billy Graham, and countless others have demonstrated the same kind of courage when it was risky or flew in the face of the status quo or politically correct law of the land. Courageous people have a "whatever it takes" mindset. When they engage with the call of God to bring life and liberation to others, massive shifts in thinking and being take place. I'm grateful for Jochebed and her courage to do whatever it took to ensure her baby's life.

Let's exercise courage to choose life, to give life and liberation to all people so that entire generations can be impacted.

The Courage to Care

Nehemiah's story is chronicled in the Old Testament book named after him. There, we read about a man who had the courage to care. Impacting a community begins with care and concern for the way things are currently.

Because of their disobedience, God had allowed the Israelites to be conquered by the Babylonians, who took the leading citizens a thousand miles away. At the time of Nehemiah, Jerusalem had been left in ruins.

Nehemiah served as cupbearer to the Babylonian king. This was more than just being a "butler." The cupbearer was sort of like a prime minister and master of ceremonies rolled into one. At each meal, he tested the king's wine and food to make sure it wasn't poisoned. If he died, then the king would know not to eat or drink what was put before him. It would take great courage just to serve in that position. A man who stood that close to the king in public had to be cultured, knowledgeable, and able to advise the king when asked. Because he had access to the king, the cupbearer was a man of great influence and impact.

God was going to use Nehemiah to help rebuild the walls of Jerusalem. That was a big deal. But how would Nehemiah get time off to lead that project? How would he get the materials needed to accomplish the feat? It was beyond Nehemiah's abilities and required more than his resources. God used Nehemiah because he expressed concern over Jerusalem and those living there:

I questioned [the men from Judah] about the Jewish remnant that had survived the exile, and also about Jerusalem. —Nehemiah 1:2b

We might think that an important man such as Nehemiah would have had greater things on his mind than a distant city and a people he had mostly never met. Yet, because his heart was for the things of God, he was focused on others and not on himself. We live in a culture that shouts, "Look out for number one! Protect your investments, line your pockets, gain control, and position yourself strategically so that you can be seen, applauded, and promoted." But the courage to care demands that we put self aside on a regular basis in order to see the needs of others and impact their situation.

Those who are hurting and struggling are often easily dismissed as someone else's responsibility or simply forgotten because of the busyness of our own schedules. Have our lives displayed evidence that we have the courage to care?

Nehemiah didn't get good news when he asked about the city:

"Those who survived the exile and are back in the province are in great trouble and disgrace. The wall of Jerusalem is broken down, and its gates have been burned with fire." —Nehemiah 1:3

Ancient city walls afforded protection against enemies. Walls kept the people and their possessions safe. Walls provided peace of mind, allowing citizens to rest a bit easier.

There are people all around us who are living vulnerable, un-protected, poverty-stricken, fearful lives. They need to know that someone cares about them. Their walls are broken. We can't burst onto the scene of their lives with the truth that God wants them to be conquerors without first showing that he cares about what they are going through.

Whom have you shown concern for this past week? this past month? God was able to use Nehemiah because he cared about the unpro-tected city. He asked questions about it. He cried over it. Then he asked God to help him do something about it. God can make a great impact through people who have the courage to care.

Nehemiah understood that God had put him in a position to do something about the broken walls of Jerusalem. He was the cup-bearer to the king, which meant he could talk to his boss about the issue. He asked for time off work and for the resources needed to rebuild the wall. That kind of request could have gotten a person killed, but if anyone could pull it off, it was the cupbearer.

When was the last time you risked anything so that someone could get the help he or she needed? What conversations have you had lately that required godly courage?

The story goes on to tell us that, although Nehemiah was courageous, he was still somewhat afraid. Courage isn't the absence of fear, but forward movement in spite of it. If we have expressed concern and felt compassion for a situation and called upon the Lord in prayer, and if God has strategically placed us in a position of influence where we can affect some kind of change, then we must move forward with God's help.

The Courage to Support

Not everyone can see potential. That's a gift, I think. I'm not just talking about a person who is positive, but a person who can see potential even when facts would argue that there is none. Perhaps you know about Barnabas, a contemporary of the Apostle Paul, who was a big encourager. Have you ever thought that it takes great courage to be an encourager?

Paul, formerly known as Saul, had been a persecutor and murderer of Christians. He was someone to be feared, not someone to follow. But Paul met the Lord personally, and he was changed. Paul had been made new. He was now one of the good guys. But not everyone would believe it. Many would be suspicious. Change takes time—or at least time to convince the skeptics.

When Paul came to Jerusalem to meet with the church leaders, they were on their guard. They were seeking out his hidden agenda. They didn't trust a guy who didn't have a trustworthy track record. Acts 9:26–30 details how Barnabas stepped up to vouch for Paul. He took Paul with him to speak to the apostles, explaining how Paul had been converted. Barnabas told them how Paul had been preaching the gospel message ever since his encounter with Jesus. It was Barnabas's courage to stand behind someone whom everyone else would have written off that enabled Paul to launch his preaching ministry. Because of Barnabas's testimony, Paul was accepted by the leaders of the church in Jerusalem.

Barnabas put his reputation on the line. He courageously vouched for someone everyone else wanted to dismiss. By faith he saw Paul's potential. He knew that Paul would be able to make a great impact on others because of his dramatic conversion. Barnabas saw, through eyes of faith, something God was doing—something that not everyone else could see at first.

There are times we need the courage to support a person or a situation even when others are hesitant.

The Courage to Lead
The fourth chapter of the Book of Judges tells us that Israel had gotten away from following the Lord (again!). This time God allowed them to become oppressed by the Canaanites. The leader of the Canaanite army was a guy named Sisera. Sisera had a lot of resources as a military commander—hundreds of chariots. And for twenty years he and his army had cruelly oppressed God's people.

During this time, a woman named Deborah was raised up by God to become judge in Israel. This was a time when there was no king. God alone was to be the people's king, but he raised up judges to administer justice and to help liberate the people whenever they got into a mess like we read about here.

I love that Deborah's office—her courtroom—was beneath a palm tree (v 5). What a cool place to meet with people!

Here's how Deborah's story goes:

She sent for Barak son of Abinoam from Kedesh in Naphtali and said to him, "The Lᴏʀᴅ, the God of Israel, commands you: 'Go, take with you ten thousand men of Naphtali and Zebulun and lead them up to Mount Tabor. I will lead Sisera, the commander of Jabin's army, with his chariots and his troops to the Kishon River and give him into your hands.' "

Barak said to her, "If you go with me, I will go; but if you don't go with me, I won't go."

"Certainly I will go with you," said Deborah. "But because of the course you are taking, the honor will not be yours, for the Lᴏʀᴅ will deliver Sisera into the hands of a woman." So Deborah went with Barak to Kedesh. There Barak summoned Zebulun and Naphtali, and ten thousand men went up under his command. Deborah also went up with him....

Then Deborah said to Barak, "Go! This is the day the Lᴏʀᴅ has given Sisera into your hands. Has not the Lᴏʀᴅ gone ahead of you?" So Barak went down Mount Tabor, with ten thousand men following him. At Barak's advance, the Lᴏʀᴅ routed Sisera and all his chariots and army by the sword, and Sisera got down from his chariot and fled on foot.

Barak pursued the chariots and army as far as Harosheth Haggoyim, and all Sisera's troops fell by the sword; not a man was left.

—Judges 4:6–10, 14–16

Deborah had the courage to lead. It's one thing to lead when things are peaceful or going well. It's quite another to lead when times are tough. Those are two different experiences entirely.

Deborah found herself leading during a period when things were bad for Israel. It was a time of war. Who wants to step up at wartime? And do we think first of a woman as the person to step up? Who knows if Deborah had ever thought, "When I grow up someday, I would really like to lead some troops into battle"? Who knows if she even saw herself as confident enough to prop up the leader of the army and support him by accompanying him to the battle line? How confidently can you go to battle when the leader of the army can't even find the courage to go? When the commanding officer is scared, what does it take to step up and speak courage into that person? Deborah did.

Deborah gave Barak a quick pep talk. She emboldened him by telling him he was going to win the battle—that God had already cleared the way for his victory. But courageous leadership is more than knowledge and more than words. When Deborah found herself having to lead beyond her role, having to go beyond where she had ever been before as a leader, she didn't hesitate. We see in the life of Deborah that leadership is more than knowing what to do. It is more than having the right answer. Courageous leaders aren't just wise. They don't just lead with words—they take action. They lead by example by going to the battle lines themselves when necessary.

Barak was paralyzed by fear. He was the commander of the army, but he couldn't even summon the courage to go to the fight. He told Deborah he would only go if she went with him. Deborah didn't say, "I'm not going that close to the battle; that's your job." She didn't say, "I'm not trained to do that." She didn't try to shame Barak into going, either. She could have called him a wimp for needing her support. But instead, she courageously stepped up to support Barak because that was what he needed to be able to follow the command of the Lord.

Courageous leaders don't sit back while people are being oppressed. Deborah had been raised up by God to do something about the situation. It was not okay with her that God's people were being mistreated. She didn't accept it as "just the way things were." She didn't merely want to do her best to lead God's people "under the circumstances." No. Courageous leaders such as

Deborah set out to change the circumstances, to make a difference, to create an impact.

Courageous leaders rely on God for direction. When Deborah laid out the military strategy for Barak, she did so after receiving that strategy from the Lord. She was bold in her words to Barak because they weren't her words. She even used the word *command* when she gave God's orders to Barak. A woman relaying a command to a man in that day and time was radical and out of the ordinary. But Deborah wasn't telling Barak what she wanted him to do. She was boldly telling him what God wanted him to do.

Are you a leader with the spirit of Deborah? Will you lead courageously to fight the battle against the powers of darkness? Will you act decisively, justly, and swiftly, and take personal risks when necessary? Will you reject the status quo and step out to help liberate people from oppression? It will take more than an awareness to make an impact. It will take more than good ideas to alter our culture. It will take men and women of courage to have the passion to lead the way for change.

The Courage to Confess

David, who became the greatest king in Old Testament Israel, was a great example of courage. He was willing to take on the giant named Goliath all by himself. But he did it with the knowledge that God was with him and that the battle was the Lord's. He knew that God would give him victory. This perspective gave him courage.

David's life was marked by victory after victory. It would have been easy for him to get a big head. It would have been tempting for him to take the credit. Songs were written about him. His fame spread quickly. He never showed fear. But like any great leader—and like all of us—David wasn't perfect. His judgment got clouded. He allowed himself to be put in a tempting situation.

One night, a woman who was bathing on the roof was right in David's line of sight. He looked longer than he should have. He was led away by evil desires and fleshly impulses. David was the king. With millions of people depending on him, with the weight of the nation on his shoulders, surely he deserved to have some pleasure. Taking someone else's wife was wrong. He knew it, but did it really matter? Her husband wasn't even home; he was off to war. What could it really hurt? No one would ever find out, right?

Second Samuel 11 tells us the result of the affair: Bathsheba became pregnant. Trying to cover up his actions, David called Bathsheba's husband, Uriah, home from the war in hopes that if they slept together, people would assume that the baby was Uriah's. Uriah came home, but he didn't sleep with his wife. Things got increasingly complicated, and the dark solution David came up with was to have Uriah murdered in battle. David basically put a hit on Uriah. Uriah died as per David's instructions, and David took Bathsheba to be his own wife.

We are told clearly what God thought about all of this:

The thing David had done displeased the Lord. —2 Samuel 11:27b

When something displeases God, he deals with it; he makes it known. God sent the prophet Nathan to confront David about his sin. David hadn't just done one wrong thing; he actually broke four commandments in one fell swoop. He coveted someone else's wife, he committed adultery, he bore false witness, and he had someone killed. But once David was confronted with his sins, he didn't make excuses or justify what he had done. He immediately and simply agreed with Nathan:

"I have sinned against the Lord." —2 Samuel 12:13a

I get the sense that from that point forward David developed a confessional lifestyle. He realized his ongoing dependence on God for cleansing. He wasn't just sorry he got caught; he was truly broken over his sin. In response, he penned some of the most beautiful, emotional, vulnerable, and humbling words in the Bible:

Have mercy on me, O God,
according to your unfailing love;
according to your great compassion
blot out my transgressions.
Wash away all my iniquity
and cleanse me from my sin.
For I know my transgressions,
and my sin is always before me.
Against you, you only, have I sinned
and done what is evil in your sight;
so you are right in your verdict
and justified when you judge. —Psalm 51:1–4

Search me, God, and know my heart;
test me and know my anxious thoughts.
See if there is any offensive way in me,
and lead me in the way everlasting. —Psalm 139:23–24

These aren't the words of someone who was trying to get away with something. In these passages we see transformation—the heart of a warrior transformed into a heart that sought after God. A macho man had become God's man.

I wonder what would have happened to David if he had not been sorry—if he had not confessed? We know that God won't be mocked. Sin is serious, and he will deal with it. But if we confess our sin, we put God and ourselves in the position for us to receive mercy.

Whoever conceals their sins does not prosper,
but the one who confesses and renounces them finds mercy.
—Proverbs 28:13

I believe David remained king only because he came clean. And because he remained king he made an undeniable impact on the nation of Israel. We can't impact this world for Christ if we cherish sin in our heart. Confession takes a lot of courage, but it is a lot easier than trying to cover our sin or argue with God.

Confess your sins to each other and pray for each other so that you may be healed. —James 5:16a

Admitting who and what we really are can be scary, but the Bible says it is the way to healing. And when we are healed we have the courage to make an impact. We can have the courage...

- ...to choose life and liberation like Jochebed, through whom people were raised up to lead and build a strong nation.

- ...to care like Nehemiah, through whom a community was restored to safety and peace.

- ...to show support like Barnabas, through whom one of the greatest Christian leaders was raised up when he could have easily been dismissed into obscurity.

- ...to lead like Deborah, through whom people were freed from oppression.

- ...to confess like David, who obtained mercy and healing and was given a second chance.

What kind of courage is God calling you to possess and display right now? God hasn't given us a spirit of timidity or fear, but one of courage (2 Timothy 1:7). We can do all things in the strength of Christ (Philippians 4:13). Christ in us is far greater than the ruler of this world, the Devil (1 John 4:4). Let's leave a mark on our culture for Christ in the power of the Spirit who gives us courage that is equal to any task.

6. Attitudes that Impact:
Adopting the Attitude of Jesus

Therefore, since Christ suffered in his body, arm yourselves also with the same attitude, because whoever suffers in the body is done with sin. As a result, they do not live the rest of their earthly lives for evil human desires, but rather for the will of God. For you have spent enough time in the past doing what pagans choose to do—living in debauchery, lust, drunkenness, orgies, carousing and detestable idolatry. They are surprised that you do not join them in their reckless, wild living, and they heap abuse on you. But they will have to give account to him who is ready to judge the living and the dead. For this is the reason the gospel was preached even to those who are now dead, so that they might be judged according to human standards in regard to the body, but live according to God in regard to the spirit.

The end of all things is near. Therefore be alert and of sober mind so that you may pray. Above all, love each other deeply, because love covers over a multitude of sins. Offer hospitality to one another without grumbling. Each of you should use whatever gift you have received to serve others, as faithful stewards of God's grace in its various forms. If anyone speaks, they should do so as one who speaks the very words of God. If anyone serves, they should do so with the strength God provides, so that in all things God may be praised through Jesus Christ. To him be the glory and the power for ever and ever. Amen. —1 Peter 4:1–11

Our attitude is critical. As Christians, we often focus on our behavior when we think about showing God's love, and we focus on our *best* behavior when we think about not sinning. But our behavior means nothing if our attitude doesn't reflect Christ.

People will often observe our attitude before they see our actions. Our behavior, designed to have a positive kingdom impact, can wind up having the opposite effect if our attitude stinks. Purity, godliness, and holiness must start on the inside.

From time to time it's important to assess ourselves and ask God to rework and remake the parts that don't yet look like Jesus. Living and loving as Jesus did involves regular self-examination. Integrity in our Christian lives means that our internal and external realities match—that we walk the talk. The passage from 1 Peter 4 describes what it means to imitate Christ and how we arm ourselves with his attitude in order to perform actions that have his impact.

Arm Yourself!

When I think of arming myself with something, I imagine having a weapon. Arming ourselves with Christ's attitude gives us the weapons we need to advance against the kingdom of darkness and to display the kingdom of light so others are convinced that God lives in us. Without a Christlike attitude, it doesn't matter how good we look on the outside. If we are critical, mean-spirited, or unkind, our squeaky-clean actions won't have a Jesus kind of impact. Our attitude can sabotage our impact for Christ in the world.

When I think of people who "have an attitude," I think of people who are cocky, maybe looking to start a fight. Perhaps they are trying to "one-up" someone or have the last word by defending themselves or justifying their actions. But the passage in 1 Peter links the attitude of Christ with suffering. Jesus was the "last word," the logos, yet he did not have a haughty, domineering kind of attitude. He accomplished everything God sent him to do without beating anyone into submission or arguing to prove a point. He accomplished God's will through suffering. He was so submitted to the Father that he accepted suffering with a godly attitude. People who strive to live like Jesus must adopt the same mindset.

Jesus suffered willingly. He never muttered under his breath, "This isn't my job!" His desire was for the will of the Father alone. He didn't come to establish a career or to make a name for himself. He came to make God's love famous and to lay down his life to save us. He didn't care if people got his title right or if he had a fancy office. He didn't care if people knew how far he had traveled to see them or if they understood how much he had studied the Scriptures or how much it cost him to spend time with them. His agenda wasn't to prove that he was right (even though he always was), but to show that God loves us and wants a relationship with us. We are supposed to adopt the same agenda by having the same attitude. We aren't here to prove to anyone that we are right. We are here to demonstrate, by our attitudes and actions, that people are loved by God—and by us.

Attitude can be defined as our internal position or feeling with regard to something or someone else. Pilots use the word *attitude* to describe a plane's horizontal relationship with the runway when landing. If their attitude isn't aligned properly, the plane will make contact with the ground at the wrong angle, causing them to crash.

In essence, your attitude is your inward disposition toward other things such as people or circumstances. Similar to the pilots' lingo, attitude is applied whenever you must deal with something or someone other than yourself. A bad attitude can cause you to clash and crash with the very people you are trying to win to Christ.

According to God's Word, when you become a Christian, a part of your new creation is the development of new attitudes:

You were taught, with regard to your former way of life, to put off your old self, which is being corrupted by its deceitful desires; to be made new in the attitude of your minds. —Ephesians 4:22–23

I'm not referring to a once-in-a-while bad mood or an occasional situation where you are tired, don't feel well, or have had a bad day and aren't much fun to be around. That happens to all of us from time to time. What I'm talking about is a pattern, a day-in-and-day-out way of relating with people, a consistent inward disposition that sees others through the lens of God's love and responds to them the way Jesus would regardless of what they say or do. When we have the right internal attitude, our actions will naturally flow out of it, and we will be able to live and love like Christ.

Paul's words admonish us to be done with sin. People who live and love with Jesus' attitude aren't led by fleshly impulses—the kinds that drive the sinful nature. In their inner attitude—the attitude of their minds and hearts—they have made the decision and declaration that they are done with sin. They aren't living for the flesh; they desire the will of God alone.

When we are armed with the attitude that we are living for God's will, we don't knee-jerk react to criticism. We don't exhibit impatience with people who don't seem to "get it." We don't flare up with anger or go into self-defense mode. We don't exert our power or authority in a fleshly "CEO" way. We aren't about image management or trying to make our plans succeed. We aren't impulsive; instead, we are prayerful and gracious.

There is a time...to be silent and a time to speak. —Ecclesiastes 3:1, 7

When we live and love like Jesus, we are aware that timing is everything. Jesus was a master at knowing when to point something out and when to say nothing. People who aren't armed with Christ's attitude are easily set off and may lash out, sound off, or argue back because in their flesh they feel a need to defend themselves, or even feel compelled to defend Christ.

Jesus constantly had reasons to be angry, to tell people off or put them in their place. He often had people taunting him, trying to get him riled up in order to discredit him. But because he was submitted to the will of God and not the flesh, he was always in control of his tongue.

Jesus never said more than was needed or more than was helpful. On several occasions, he said nothing. When he did display anger, there was a righteous reason, and the power of God was on display. What kind of impact could we have on people and circumstances if we prayed, "Lord, help me never say more than is needed or more than will be helpful"?

Everyone should be quick to listen, slow to speak and slow to become angry. —James 1:19b

Anger, self-defense, and the need to be right keep the flesh stirred up. I can't think of anyone I have ever met who said it was their goal to become and stay as angry as possible because they just loved how it made them feel.

Those who belong to Christ Jesus have crucified the flesh with its passions and desires. —Galatians 5:24

We become dead to the flesh and its demand for attention, its need to be fed with anger and defensiveness, when we submit completely to the will of God. In the process, we will become absolutely "done with sin."

Sin isn't just about breaking a commandment; it's about missing the mark. If we sabotage what God might want to do in a situation because of a bad attitude, I believe we need to consider it sin and repent.

Be Transformed
People who desire the attitude of Jesus sign up for transformation. They want to change. In order to live and love with the temperament of Jesus, there must be an inner work going on that will sustain and enable the outer work we do. If we sign up for it, we must

surrender to it. We must present ourselves in our bodies to God by saying *no* to the flesh and *yes* to the Spirit. We must present ourselves in our minds by allowing God to transform our thoughts and attitudes. And we must offer our spirits to God so that deep within they are being transformed and we automatically think and act and live as Jesus did. That's how we live according to God in our spirit. If we live this way, Christ's attitude will become automatic because it is seared into our souls.

Signing up for transformation is the only way we can arm ourselves with Jesus' attitude because all of us have triggers. Each of us has a button people can push. Each of us has character flaws, shortcomings, and personality challenges. The good news is we can absolutely be made new. Rough edges can become smooth, short tempers can be stayed, critical spirits can become filled with grace. But we must acknowledge that we aren't perfect and submit ourselves to transformation.

Attaining spiritual maturity is more than having a growing or advanced knowledge of the Bible. It involves a maturing of our character, our inner self, which will enable us to be self-controlled, patient, loving, gentle, and kind. It starts with an attitude that desires to submit to that process.

People who live with Jesus' attitude keep their minds free from clutter, and they keep themselves in check through prayer. Getting Jesus' attitude right is tied to our ability to stop and listen and talk with God. It's connected to regularly de-cluttering our lives of the voices that compete for our attention. It's focusing on the voice of God alone so we aren't confused by worldly wisdom and human principles and practices. It's about being self-controlled so that we don't run ahead of God.

Prayer is like a speed bump between our impulses and God's plans. We "check ourselves" when we pray. Not only do we pray for wisdom and help, but we also ask God to show us who we are or where we have failed. When his Spirit reveals the answers to us, we are able to change our attitudes and alter our course. It's often in the place of prayer that God's transforming work is done because in prayer, God transmits his thoughts to us. This gives us a different perspective on our situation than we had previously, and it changes our course of action.

It is also through prayer that we gain victory over the flesh and find power to live as those who are truly done with sin. No one was more focused and clear-minded than Jesus:

Jesus often withdrew to lonely places and prayed. —Luke 5:16

Jesus knew exactly what the Father wanted him to do because he was regularly in communication with him.

Be Generous
People who live and love with Jesus' attitude are generous with others. Generosity has a positive impact on people. Our call is to stay above the fray, above the drama. Our call is to love and serve. We lead the way for harmony, unity, and transformation in people's lives when we choose love. When we choose to love, we give the benefit of the doubt and thank God for those people who require "extra grace" from us. As long as you are living, there will always be certain people who tend to drive you nuts, but to dismiss or avoid them isn't Christlike. Those with the attitude of Jesus don't look for a quick way to pawn people and their needs off on others when they could share the love of Christ themselves.

Jesus was generous with people. Great transformation came into people's lives just because he gave them time and attention, and they knew he genuinely wanted to. Some people are only going to change as they see Christ demonstrated in your attitude. They may not know that they need to change or ought to change unless they spend time with someone who is living the life of Christ, someone who can help them see there is a better way.

It's a lot more fun to love others to Jesus than it is to try to be their judge and tell them everything you think they ought to change. Even when God uses us to speak truth to people and challenge them to a different way of life, it is supposed to be done in love (see Ephesians 4:15).

When we arm ourselves with Christ's attitude, we can learn to overlook some things. I'm not talking about overlooking sin. I'm just talking about giving grace to people, not keeping a record of offenses, and giving people the benefit of the doubt.

A Christlike attitude will lead to hospitality. We display Jesus' attitude when we serve even when no one is looking and when we do it with a joyful heart without thinking, "Why am I the one doing this? I'm already busy enough." Hospitality isn't about serving only when it's convenient or when we've had time to clean the house and clear our schedules. It's about being available to people even when it requires sacrifice. Remember, the attitude of Jesus is also an attitude of sacrifice.

People who live and love with Jesus' attitude are ready to dispense grace. Isn't that what Christianity is all about? We live and teach the truth, and we hand out grace. When we wake up each morning, we ought to put our feet on the floor and say, "Today, I am going to live and teach the truth of Jesus' love and hand out as much grace as possible, using everything God has given me and every opportunity that comes my way." Sometimes that's tough to keep in the front of our thinking when we are cut off in traffic or someone calls the wrong number the third time in a row. It is challenging when we open the drive-thru bag and the cheeseburger that was supposed to have ketchup only has every other possible condiment smeared all over it. People make mistakes. Every gift we have received becomes a tool for dispensing God's grace to others.

Our gifts enable God's grace to be experienced. We ought to be like little Pez dispensers of grace; whenever we open our mouths, grace should pop out. Why? When grace flows into people's lives, they are attracted to the source of that grace and are changed.

Grace transforms culture because it transforms people. Don't we know that to be true? Haven't we received grace? Haven't we been given second chances? Haven't we botched a few things and needed another opportunity? Haven't we been on the wrong path and had a friend come lovingly alongside of us, put a hand on our shoulder, pray for us, and help us turn around? Haven't we had our sins forgiven and our slates wiped clean?

We've all needed grace, and those of us who have experienced it get to live and minister as Jesus by giving it out to those who haven't yet been freed by it. We have what the world needs to hear! People are tired of the judgment and labels that religion has placed on them. They are ready for some words of grace and assurance:

"Though your sins are like scarlet,
they shall be as white as snow." —Isaiah 1:18b

People are thirsty for the life-giving words that their past can become past and all things can become new. They are longing to hear the news that God sees them as they are and loves them perfectly regardless of their life's circumstance.

There are some behaviors we overlook in children because they are children. It's not that we don't take time to instruct them during teachable or private moments, but sometimes kids act the way they do because that's the way kids act. We ought not be shocked by the behavior of sinners or even some Christians who are still young in the faith. There is a time and a place to lovingly instruct someone that doesn't involve harsh judgment and criticism. Criticism isn't going to compel people to change, but grace will.

People who live and love with Christ's attitude speak God's words into people's lives. It is God's wisdom that we draw on. If we haven't heard it from God, we don't need to pass it on. Our opinions aren't going to help anyone, but God's Word can deliver and rescue people from every trouble. Jesus only shared that which God instructed him to say (John 12:49).

People who live and love with Christ's attitude don't rely on themselves; instead, they rely on God's strength. When we find ourselves operating in our own strength, it's not too long before we're stressed, anxious, restless, and tired—a condition that can create a negative attitude. There is an ease, however, to life and to ministry when we are flowing in God's power. Call upon the Holy Spirit to give you the strength and ability to strive with people, to pursue peace with people, to seek to bless people.

Those who have Christ's attitude aren't attempting to make a name for themselves, but are trying to draw attention to God through Jesus Christ so God will receive the glory.

Perhaps today can be one of those "take a hard look at myself" days for you:

- Is your attitude such that people see Jesus in your life?
- Have you determined to be done with sin and decided that you want God's will alone?
- Are you being changed on the inside, or are you holding on to what needs to change by justifying your actions?
- Are you praying for change?
- Are you praying for Jesus' attitude?
- Are you showing love and hospitality?
- Are you giving people the benefit of the doubt?

- Are you willing to overlook some things in order to give grace to people who really need Jesus?

- Are you relying on God's power or your own strength?

- Is it your desire to show Jesus off in every situation?

May God help us impact the world for him through the adoption of Jesus' attitude.

7. A Generational Impact:
Inspiring Faith in Others

These are the commands, decrees and laws the LORD your God directed me to teach you to observe in the land that you are crossing the Jordan to possess, so that you, your children and their children after them may fear the LORD your God as long as you live by keeping all his decrees and commands that I give you, and so that you may enjoy long life. Hear, Israel, and be careful to obey so that it may go well with you and that you may increase greatly in a land flowing with milk and honey, just as the LORD, the God of your ancestors, promised you.

Hear, O Israel: The LORD our God, the LORD is one. Love the LORD your God with all your heart and with all your soul and with all your strength. These commandments that I give you today are to be on your hearts. Impress them on your children. Talk about them when you sit at home and when you walk along the road, when you lie down and when you get up. Tie them as symbols on your hands and bind them on your foreheads. Write them on the doorframes of your houses and on your gates.

When the LORD your God brings you into the land he swore to your fathers, to Abraham, Isaac and Jacob, to give you—a land with large, flourishing cities you did not build, houses filled with all kinds of good things you did not provide, wells you did not dig, and vineyards and olive groves you did not plant—then when you eat and are satisfied, be careful that you do not forget the LORD, who brought you out of Egypt, out of the land of slavery. —Deuteronomy 6:1–12

Transforming culture is a large and lengthy process. Turning the tide of opinion and behavior and shaping the hearts of many takes a collision of gigantic proportions. It takes a collective commitment and collaborative effort. In order to effect real change, the hearts and minds of an entire generation need to be impacted. What can we do as individuals to impress those who are coming behind us to choose God and his ways? How will the hearts of future generations be turned away from self and worldly wisdom and toward Christ and his call to follow a different agenda?

The Israelites were to follow the commands of God so that those coming behind them—their children and grandchildren—would also be inclined to make the same choices. Obviously, children grow up and make their own choices. Your obedience to Christ is not a guarantee that your children and grandchildren will make the same choice, but it has the power to pull them in that direction. Disobedience to Christ, conversely, has the power to push them away. What we model matters.

This passage in Deuteronomy speaks about enjoying a long life. This was not talking specifically about the exact number of years the Israelites would live, but about God establishing them in the Promised Land. He had given them a new place to work and enjoy, and the prerequisite for enjoying that land and the blessings of God for a long time was obedience to God.

It is my observation that many young people growing up today are more confused than ever about who they are and why they are here. There is an aimlessness, an attitude of "settling" rather than a desire to conquer and be established in this life. God never wanted his people to settle for anything less than the Promised Land. They were to have a conquering, confident, "can-do" spirit that would lead them to be the established people of God.

Who's Watching You?

Those coming behind us are watching our lives. Are we tenacious, courageous, and willing to take the Promised Land God has called us to occupy? Or have we settled for something less than God's best for our lives? Have we had a "take-what-we-can-get" attitude rather than a "taking-the-Promised-Land" attitude?

Being planted by God in the Promised Land would bring the Israelites a time of increase; things would go well for them if they obeyed the Lord. Don't we want that for our children? Don't we want to see them established in life? Don't we want them to enjoy it? Don't we want them to see blessing and increase? How we choose to live in relationship with God demonstrates what that looks like. What we model matters. If we aren't living an abundant life, why should we expect those coming behind us to choose to follow in our footsteps?

I'm not suggesting that obedience to God means Christians will live wealthy and trouble-free lives. But obedient believers experience wellness, energy, vitality, strength, peace, joy, contentment, and a God-given favor that people who are disconnected from God's work do not experience. I see this a lot with people who are up and down in their Christian walk. They will have six months of peace and calm and joy and then quit coming to church for four months. Their social media posts will be riddled with drama and doubt. Their lives will spin out of control, their relationships will be on-again-off-again, and they will sink into a depressed and withdrawn state. Once they have had enough of that and they reconnect with the presence of God, things slowly start to turn around—until the time they disconnect again and wonder why things are so up and down for them.

Obedience isn't something that is on-again, off-again. It is consistent. It is a faithful pursuit. It is not a perfect pursuit, but a faithful one. Our children and those who come behind us need to see a committed, steady pursuit of the things of God. This generation is more skeptical than any previous generation. They don't just take our word for it because we are adults. They want to see it walked out in our lives. Are we giving them a reason to want to walk in our footsteps?

Our Passion

Deuteronomy 6:5 is really the pinnacle of all of God's commands:

Love the LORD your God with all your heart and with all your soul and with all your strength.

Does such an attitude characterize your walk with Christ? Are you making every effort to press into your relationship with God with all of your being? Does your passion for Christ make the young people you have a relationship with want to be better Christians?

If attending church regularly isn't important to us, how can we think it should be someday for our children? If reading the Bible and relying on it for life's answers isn't modeled in front of our children, how can we expect them to turn to the Word of God when they are in crisis? If tithing, giving offerings, and being generous with people in need isn't a priority in our lives, how will our children learn to be good friends and neighbors to others? If we aren't engaged in the worship of God, what does our lack of participation say to the onlooking generation? Do our children know how to pray because we have taught them how to call on God? Do they witness us going to the Lord to intercede for others or to seek guidance for our own lives and families?

Dads and moms, grandparents, aunts and uncles, pastors, leaders, teachers, coaches, anyone who influences children—what you model matters! Your commitment to the Lord can inspire the next generation.

Our Time

Our personal time makes a great impact. It's time for us to have some good old-fashioned conversations. Not just a quick text. Not a convenient press of a "like" button on Facebook. Not a hurried "How was your day?" or "Do you have any homework?" It's time for some focused, intentional talk. It's time for spiritual conversations where we impress some things on our children.

Do our children know the Ten Commandments and the meaning behind them? Are we teaching our children to value all people and to value life? Are we impressing on our children the meaning of our words and actions? Do we talk about what it means to be a Christian family or to serve the Lord, to be people of impact? Do our children know the key themes in the Scriptures? Are we teaching them to make good decisions based on the principles in God's Word?

Deuteronomy commands constant conversation—an ongoing dialogue between parents and their children. Spiritual matters should be part of the fabric of a family's dynamic. Whether we are coming or going, whether it is in the morning or the evening, the family should be engaged in conversations regarding the commands of the Scriptures and the relationship God wants to have with his people.

Real conversation takes time, and it has to happen on purpose. Who are you taking time to talk with about things that really matter? Even if you don't have children living at home, you can make time for a young person in this generation. What if we identified two or three young people with whom we could spend one hour a week? Imagine how that one hour could turn into a relationship of great impact. What conversations could flow from an intentional investment in the life of a young person?

What we model matters. The way we spend our time matters. Are we taking the time to actually impact the younger generation, or are they growing up without role models and without necessary, life-preparing conversations? Are our children falling into temptation and getting into trouble because we haven't prepared them to face life's challenges?

Time is something we can't save. We either invest it or we lose it. It is the greatest resource we have. Young people need mentors, people who will invest time in them. I challenge all of us to look for ways, whether we have children living at home or not, to spend time with the children of this generation. You can volunteer at an elementary school. You can coach a sports team. You can be a camp counselor. You can be a tutor. You can be an after-school caregiver. You can pick a child up and bring him or her to church. (Even car conversations can be impactful!) You could take a child in need shopping and just spoil him or her for a few hours.

In order for children to hear and receive our words, they need our time. How many hours this past week did you spend in conversation with someone younger than you in an effort to influence that person in a positive way? Imagine the impact we could have on the next generation if each of us would spend a little time and lead by example.

Thankful Living

One important characteristic of the Christian life that is often overlooked is the discipline of thanksgiving. A spirit of thanksgiving can point people to God as our source. God reminded the Israelites of how he had taken them out of a bad place and put them in a place filled with opportunity and blessing. Making sure your children know the abundance of good things that come from God is a way to impact them. Help them realize that, if they are able to develop a skill, it is because God has gifted them. If they are able to be gainfully employed, it is because God has opened the door. Point them to the realization that the things they acquire and achieve are because God has made it possible. Developing the attitude and understanding that God owns all and is the one who gives to us so we can *receive* a blessing and *be* a blessing is important in helping this next generation live well. Remembering the Lord and his provision goes a long way toward helping people keep right priorities in life.

I am not sure what grade my own children would give me as a mom. I would have to award myself top marks as the family "taxi driver"—I think I do that one pretty well. I also think I score high in the area of acknowledging God. Whether it is a more expensive Christmas gift than we might usually get for them, a special trip we have been able to take, or even a fancy meal out, I often remind our children that what they are experiencing is the blessing of God. What could inspire young people to follow God more than to know that he is the one who blesses their lives? When you forget to acknowledge God, you cut off your source.

In addition to being thankful and constantly acknowledging God, telling the stories of how God has delivered us, met us, supplied for us, and seen us through is also crucial. The children in our lives need to hear our God-stories. If you are in Christ, do your children know how and when you were saved? Have you told them of the times he has answered prayer? Have you shared with them how your life was before you met Christ so that they can see the true impact Jesus has made? Do they know how he has changed you?

Your personal walk, your personal time, and your personal testimony have power. God wants you to use them to collide with the culture and impact this generation of young people who are gaining identity, values, and spiritual insight from your life and mine.

8. An Everywhere Impact:
An Evangelism Lifestyle

While a large crowd was gathering and people were coming to Jesus from town after town, he told this parable: "A farmer went out to sow his seed. As he was scattering the seed, some fell along the path; it was trampled on, and the birds ate it up. Some fell on rocky ground, and when it came up, the plants withered because they had no moisture. Other seed fell among thorns, which grew up with it and choked the plants. Still other seed fell on good soil. It came up and yielded a crop, a hundred times more than was sown." —Luke 8:4–8a

Jesus often spoke in parables to help people understand principles such as discipleship, loving our neighbor, being faithful stewards, the kingdom of God, and salvation. In this parable in Luke 8, Jesus is the farmer. We see him sowing seed everywhere. He was always on a mission to sow seed. It didn't matter if he was on a path, near the rocks, in the thorns, or on good soil. The farmer scattered seed everywhere.

We read about some seed that fell on the path and was trampled on and eaten by birds. Some seed fell on rocky soil, which prevented the plants from putting down roots. Some fell among thorns and got choked out while trying to grow. Even though the seed didn't grow well in these three places, it was still scattered there.

God is keenly aware that not everyone will receive the seed of the gospel, although it is sown in all kinds of places through all kinds of strategies and methods. There are many reasons why people reject the good news and keep Jesus at a distance. Many won't accept the seed of the gospel when it is sown, but *some* will. And because some will, it is worth making every effort to scatter the seed of the gospel as often as possible and in as many places as possible. The effort is worth it for those who will accept it and allow it to be planted firmly in their hearts.

Rather than think of the path, the rocks, and the thorns as representing people's readiness to accept the gospel, let's think of them as the places you and I are called to go in order to make sure the seed of the gospel falls in as many places as possible. I am afraid we have become skittish about sowing seed just anywhere. Sometimes, we like to pick and choose the places where we will get involved. We are wary of where we invest our time, effort, and resources, if we are willing to sow the seed of the gospel at all.

The Hard Path

Maybe the path represents a difficult place for you to think about going. Perhaps it is difficult to think about ministering to people in a homeless shelter or to those living on the streets. Maybe it is daunting to think of talking to hookers, strippers, drug addicts, or alcoholics about Jesus. Could you picture yourself going into the rough parts of your community armed with the good news about Jesus? Would that be difficult for you?

In what ways is your church committed to engaging people on the hard path with the love of Jesus, with the good news of his resurrection from the dead? Do we even need to be engaged with people on the hard path? Aren't there plenty of people on the easy path, people who live lives like us, who also need Jesus? I mean, we work hard, make honest choices, and love our families. Aren't there lots of people like us we could witness to? Why stretch to minister to those on the path?

The path is a hard, and sometimes seemingly impossible, place to minister. It's obviously not the most receptive environment. Don't we want to labor in fields we think can produce the most fruit for the Kingdom? Why should we reach to witness on the path? The reason is that, although some will never accept the good news of the gospel, some will. And for the some who will, isn't it worth going into the dark places, into the hard places, to make sure these people reach heaven? Shouldn't we do it for the some?

Maybe you were once hard-headed and traveling on the hard road, walking in the way of darkness and addiction, and someone sowed some seed in your path. Aren't you grateful that someone stepped away from comfort long enough to intersect with your path, to scatter a little bit of the love of Jesus in front of you?

My husband was one of those on the hard path before we met. He had sold out to a lifestyle of drugs and alcohol from the time he was sixteen until he was twenty-six. Even though he had been raised in church, even though he had given his life to the Lord at a young age, even though he had been a leader early on in his youth group, he veered off course, choosing a hard life for an entire decade. But a Southern Baptist preacher saw something in him and went against the odds to go after him on the path. In one weekend, my husband was delivered from addiction and was enrolled in seminary to train to become a Christian counselor.

Why not take some living water onto the path and pour it at someone's feet so that the seed of the gospel will have a chance to take root in that person's life? Do it for the some.

The Rocks

Let's allow the rocks to represent a place of great faith and great effort. I've only tried rock climbing a few times—when I was much younger. It wasn't pretty, and the helmet I had to wear gave me "helmet-hair" for the rest of the day. Rock climbing was not only a fashion killer, but it was also exhausting. Not knowing where to step and straining to pull myself up, never knowing when I would actually reach the summit, was mentally and physically draining. Even though I was making progress, it always seemed as if I was eternally far from the top. I never felt as if I was getting anywhere, yet I was expending tremendous energy, and at times I felt uncertain and afraid. Could I keep going? Would I ever make it to the top?

Maybe you have been expending great effort to minister to someone on the rocky path. Maybe you have tried to befriend someone who needs Jesus and you've invited this person to church over and over and over again. You've modeled servanthood and generosity and the love of Christ. You've prayed for this person and started spiritual conversations, but it seems that you aren't getting anywhere. Maybe this person wears you out by seeming one minute to be getting this "Jesus stuff" and wanting to make progress, but the next minute going back to living for himself or herself and obeying the voice of Satan. There are spurts of forward progress, but no real long-term commitment. As a pastor, I deal with this kind of person often. I know it is exhausting. I know it is difficult.

Why continue to reach and stretch and talk and hope and pray? Because *some* will finally have their rocky, stubborn hearts busted into pieces and will be transformed into pliable people who are filled with the Spirit of God. Keep climbing those rocks looking for places to scatter some seed. Why not take the Word of God with you and break up some of those rocks, shatter some of the lies of the Enemy, and scatter the gospel? Even in the rocky places, some seed will fall into a crack in the rocks where it can take root. Do it for the some.

The Thorns

I would suggest that the thorns represent the sticky, prickly, hard-to-get-to places around us. It may feel increasingly difficult to represent the Lord in our public schools. It may be difficult in our workplaces to let our light shine with the good news that Jesus makes a difference in our lives. I'm afraid our political correctness has caused us to adopt the philosophy that we are to mind our own business. But that's not what Jesus commanded us to do. He has told us to mind *his* business, and his business is the spreading of the good news of the gospel and the love of God. Jesus didn't say, "I came to mind my own business." He said, "I came to do my Father's business" (Luke 2:49).

Oh, I know. We can get hurt in thorny places. It hurts to be pricked by thorns, to be persecuted for sowing the gospel seed in thorny areas, to be labeled and rejected. Why put ourselves in harm's way? Why set ourselves up for ridicule? Many in thorny places aren't likely to receive the gospel. But some will. Do it for the some.

Determined to Sow

The church of the living God is supposed to be an army on a mission. The mission is to win souls for the kingdom of God. The mission is to deliver people from the strong grip of the enemy. Can you picture a soldier telling his commanding officer that he would like to skip being assigned to the path because it is too out in the open where he would be an easy target? Or that he would like to skip the rocks because it would be too easy for him to fall and would be an exhausting location to serve? Or could he please not have to deal with thorny terrain because he wouldn't want to get caught on a briar? Requests such as that in the military would not only be absurd, but they would earn you more discomfort than any assignment of service ever could.

When soldiers are on a mission, they serve wherever they find themselves. Their job is to protect and liberate people and to take out the enemy—whether that's on a hard, dusty path or on a jagged, rocky cliff or in a thorny, prickly patch. They don't wait to carry out their mission until they reach lush pastures or the comfort of an air-conditioned space. They do what they are commanded to do wherever they are sent, because they never know when someone will need to be rescued in that place of service.

In Acts 17, the Apostle Paul was in Athens, a large metropolis in the ancient world. Athens was a tough place to minister. It was rocky, hard, and thorny all at the same time. There was nothing easy about preaching in Athens. The city was full of idols—probably over a thousand different ones. But Paul didn't go to Athens to see the sights. He went to win some souls for Jesus' sake. He wasn't just passing through. He went there on purpose. He knew that the people of Athens were a "hot mess" when it came to the mixed bag of religion they espoused, but he went there anyway.

There were two main schools of thought in Athens. There were the Epicureans, who thought the key to spirituality was found through living it up. They wanted the finest things in life. They pursued pleasure. For them, religion was all about personal experience and feeling good. They were materialists to the max. They treated their pain, their confusion, and their questions by piling on more and more sensual pleasures. Their motto was, "Enjoy life." Don't we live in a time where the mindset of the Epicureans rules? What an empty philosophy.

The second group was the Stoics. Their emphasis was on self-discipline and self-control. They were committed to reason and self-reliance, and they strived to be unmoved by feelings and ambivalent toward outward circumstances. Pride ruled for the Stoics; they always saw themselves as in total control. Their motto was, "Endure life." It is interesting that the first two leaders of Stoicism committed suicide. Relying on self doesn't work.

Paul didn't just walk into this hotbed of spiritual confusion and hope for the best. In order to scatter seed wisely, Paul had to know some things. He had to understand some things. He had to learn some things about how these groups thought, what they believed, and how they viewed life and eternity. He couldn't bury his head in the cultural sand if he was going to be a preacher of the gospel. He had to know his audience. He had to understand the culture. Paul had to do his homework before he could scatter the seed of the gospel if he was to have any hope for success.

Being Equipped

What about us? Are we equipping ourselves to more effectively scatter seed? How many of us know someone who is Jewish, Jehovah's Witness, Mormon, Hindu, Muslim, Buddhist, atheist, deist, or agnostic? Have we taken the approach that it's best just to not talk religion with these people? Or are we learning about their beliefs and philosophies so that we can thoughtfully engage them in dialogue? It's not enough to just know what *we* believe as Christians. If we are going to engage this culture for Christ, we need to know what other religions are espousing. Not every Mormon or Muslim you befriend will turn to the truth of Christ, but some will. Do it for the some.

If you want to reach drug addicts for Jesus, why not do some reading on how to reach addicts? Wouldn't it be helpful to know how addicts tend to think? what they believe about the way to happiness? how they experience and process life through their thoughts and feelings? There are observable patterns that addicts share. When you understand those patterns, you can talk to addicts in ways that will help them connect with their need for the gospel. Addiction is hard. The voice of the drug is compelling and commanding. Not every addict you engage will walk away from the escape the drug provides in the moment in order to turn to Jesus for the long term—but some will. We must engage the addicts for the *some* who will be rescued for Jesus' sake.

Prompted by the Spirit of God, I began reading and asking more questions of and about the homosexual population. I wanted to know how to effectively minister to those in this ever-increasing, diverse, and open group. I wanted to do my homework—not only to have knowledge and tools but to also have understanding so that I could compassionately offer a different approach to life, through following Jesus, that was compelling. I wanted to give people hope and evidence that it is possible to live with sexual purity regardless of what you believe about your orientation.

Those who identify as homosexuals but who choose not to practice in order to faithfully follow Jesus deal with an intense loneliness that many of us cannot understand. If marriage was God's solution to Adam's loneliness and marriage is supposed to be a picture of Christ and his church, then the church is supposed to be a solution to people's loneliness today. If we want to see some come out of that lifestyle and embrace the grace and mercy of Christ, we had better step up to the plate and offer authentic, encouraging friendship to people who struggle with homosexuality.

Angie Williams is a woman in our congregation who understands the pain of loneliness. She was in her mid-thirties when she found herself single and pregnant. She was isolated from her church—and not by her choice. A few years ago, she began a ministry to single moms that has had a profound impact on many, many women as they have found God's grace to help them in their time of need. Angie knows how these women think. She knows their fears. She understands what it is like to be alone in that situation. She is engaging women with the love of Jesus at their point of need. They need friendship. They need support. They need some mentoring. They need car seats and diapers. As they receive those things through our "Heartbeat of the Valley" educational and supportive ministry, they will see the true love of Jesus. And as they experience the love of Jesus, some will discover their need for his love and desire to belong to him. Yes, some will take the training classes, acquire their cribs and car seats, and be on their way. But some will accept Jesus as Savior. Angie is doing what she is doing for the some.

One year, on "Sanctity of Life Sunday," we invited all of the single moms in our program to come to church. We incentivized them by telling them we would give them a gas card if they attended. Some came—and it was chaotic. They sat on the front row with all of their babies and toddlers. There were kids running everywhere, hanging off the altars and playing with trucks on the floor. There were attempts to take the platform and to run all over the front of the sanctuary. But we were so glad they were there. The week after their visit, I opened Facebook to read this from one of the visiting moms:

Pastor Melissa, I wanted to take a moment to truly thank you for welcoming me last Sunday into your church family. It was the first time in many years I've felt comfortable being in a church environment. My last experience at a church was when I was fourteen years old and had a necklace ripped from my neck. I was told I wasn't old enough to have the privilege to wear a cross with Christ on it. I never went back. Being with you guys, I truly felt the Spirit of Christ in your house of the Lord. I am excited to be coming more to your Sunday services and having my children involved in a church family. So, from the bottom of my heart, thank you for giving me the chance to have a new church family and allowing me to get closer to our Heavenly Father again. After attending for a while, I'd love to be baptized and have my children dedicated like you did for the children last Sunday until they are ready to be baptized themselves.

How many single moms were invited to that special service? About thirty. How many came? Five. But for the one who encountered Christ, her life will never, ever be the same. That is impact. That is a lasting mark.

Now, let's go back to Acts 17. Paul had done his homework. He was ready to take on people who were convinced that their way of life was the way to live. With the attention of all present, Paul had his turn to speak:

"People of Athens! I see that in every way you are very religious. For as I walked around and looked carefully at your objects of worship, I even found an altar with this inscription: TO AN UNKNOWN GOD. So you

are ignorant of the very thing you worship—and this is what I am going to proclaim to you.

"The God who made the world and everything in it is the Lord of heaven and earth and does not live in temples built by human hands. And he is not served by human hands, as if he needed anything. Rather, he himself gives everyone life and breath and everything else. From one man he made all the nations, that they should inhabit the whole earth; and he marked out their appointed times in history and the boundaries of their lands. God did this so that they would seek him and perhaps reach out for him and find him, though he is not far from any one of us. 'For in him we live and move and have our being.' As some of your own poets have said, 'We are his offspring.'

"Therefore since we are God's offspring, we should not think that the divine being is like gold or silver or stone—an image made by human design and skill. In the past God overlooked such ignorance, but now he commands all people everywhere to repent. For he has set a day when he will judge the world with justice by the man he has appointed. He has given proof of this to everyone by raising him from the dead." —Acts 17:22b–31

Paul masterfully acknowledged where the Athenians were and connected with them and their culture. Too often we want to start the conversation with the gospel rather than engage people where they are. When Adam sinned in the Garden of Eden, God didn't come to him with the blood of an animal and animal skin to cover his nakedness first. He came to him with a question:

"Where are you?" —Genesis 3:9b

God wanted Adam to evaluate where he found himself. He wanted Adam to see the futility of living life his own way. He wanted Adam to take note that he was sitting in shame and that he was now living in fear and in hiding. He wanted Adam to discover that who he had become wasn't who he was created to be and that he could no longer be authentic and open with God. He wanted Adam to acknowledge that he was broken, that sin had destroyed something wonderful. He wanted Adam to see how sin had dislocated him from God.

When you seek to minister to people who are caught in a lifestyle of sin and who embrace a different way of thinking and living from that which the Bible teaches, consider starting with some questions. Ask them about their religion. For the Muslim, ask about how he came to the conclusion that following Allah is the right way to live. For the addict, ask her when her drug use started and if she ever thinks of leaving that life behind. If you are convinced for Christ yourself, his Spirit will guide your words.

Paul scattered the seed of the gospel in hard, pride-filled, rocky, thorny Athens. And look at the result:

When they heard about the resurrection of the dead, some of them sneered, but others said, "We want to hear you again on this subject." At that, Paul left the Council. Some of the people became followers of Paul and believed. —Acts 17:32–34a

Some dismissed what Paul said entirely. Some were open to future dialogue. And some believed. Paul did it for the some and for the possibility that some more would follow. How powerful! Paul lived his life to obey Jesus' command to preach the gospel for the some who would believe.

Here was Paul's approach to all of this:

Though I am free and belong to no one, I have made myself a slave to everyone, to win as many as possible. To the Jews I became like a Jew, to win the Jews. To those under the law I became like one under the law (though I myself am not under the law), so as to win those under the law. To those not having the law I became like one not having the law (though I am not free from God's law but am under Christ's law), so as to win those not having the law. To the weak I became weak, to win the weak. I have become all things to all people so that by all possible means I might save some.

—1 Corinthians 9:19–22

Paul did it for the *some*. We are called to scatter the seed of the gospel everywhere. As we do, some will mock Jesus. Some will reject him. Some will dismiss him. But some will receive him. *Do it for the some.*

9. A Prayerful Impact:
A Strategy for Transformation

"As for me, far be it from me that I should sin against the LORD by failing to pray for you." —1 Samuel 12:23a

When you hear the name of the Apostle Paul, what comes to your mind? Is it his dynamic conversion on the road to Damascus, when God changed him from being a persecutor and murderer of believers into a dynamic Christian and a powerhouse for the gospel? Maybe you think of Paul's incredible church planting prowess and effective preaching as he went from town to town to establish new congregations. Maybe it was the way he revisited those churches from time to time to see how they were doing and to give them instruction, correction, or encouragement. Perhaps you think of the thirteen wonderful books in the New Testament that Paul gave us. Maybe what comes to your mind is the way he mentored Timothy and others to become pastors themselves. What an accomplished person Paul was. What a spiritual giant. What a transformational, soul-winning, and passionate man of great impact.

While people were no doubt impressed by Paul's fervor, attention, mentoring, writing, and preaching, I believe none of those things would have had the impact they did without Paul's commitment to prayer. Countless times in his writings, Paul shared prayers or mentioned what he was praying about, particularly as he prayed for the people who had heard his sermons. Everything he said as he preached, everything he said as he instructed churches and leaders, everywhere he went—all of it was bathed in prayer. Prayer does more than leave an initial impression. It makes a lasting impact on the lives of people because the Spirit of God gets involved when we pray for others.

Paul wasn't ashamed to tell people he was praying for them. He understood that the ministry of prayer is one way God pursues people. People need to know that they are so important to God, and to you, that you spend time investing in them through the ministry of prayer. This is a powerful thing! I don't hesitate to tell people I am praying that they will get back into church, that they will be healed, or that they will come to faith in Christ. I can't tell you how much it means to me to get e-mails or texts from people, or to have them come to me personally, to let me know they are praying for me. Not even considering what God can do when we pray, but just knowing that someone cares enough about me to lift me to the Father in prayer, lifts my spirits immediately.

Doctors, why not let your patients know that, in addition to providing medical treatment based on sound knowledge and experience, you will also pray for them? Teachers, in addition to telling your students your policies on late homework and tardiness, why not let them know that you are a person who prays and that you will pray for them to have a successful school year?

Why not utilize social media to let people know you will pray for them? There is no shortage of prayer opportunities on Facebook and Twitter. In any given week, someone will:

- lose a loved one or a pet.
- be laid off from a job.
- interview for a job.
- receive unexpected health news.
- deal with an unexpected injury.

- ask for prayer for a missing person or wayward child.

- share about a huge test coming up.

- need to make a critical decision.

- break up with a girlfriend or boyfriend.

- have a fight with a friend.

- lose something important.

- fail to make the team.

- simply have a bad day.

Why not take a moment to pray and message someone? Let that person know that his or her need matters to God and to you.

What Paul Prayed

Not only was Paul not ashamed to tell people he was praying for them, but he also wasn't ashamed to disclose the content of his prayers for them. He told others what he said when he talked to God on their behalf. We know because he wrote his thoughts down. What would people think of the content of *our* prayers? If someone sat and listened to you pray and wrote down all that you said, would the record include the kind of instruction, encouragement, and Holy Spirit power (1 Corinthians 2:4) that Paul's prayers did? Let's look at some of the content of Paul's prayers, and perhaps gain a strategy for leaving a lasting impact in the lives of others through our own prayers.

Thanksgiving

Paul would often tell God that he was thankful for people when he prayed. People weren't a burden to Paul, but a blessing; it was a privilege for him to take them before the Lord in prayer:

I thank my God through Jesus Christ for all of you, because your faith is being reported all over the world. God, whom I serve in my spirit in preaching the gospel of his Son, is my witness how constantly I remember you in my prayers at all times. —Romans 1:8–10a

It had to be a blessing for Paul to see fruit for his labor, to see people really getting grounded in Christ and going on to share the good news of the resurrection personally instead of them just sitting back and expecting Paul to be God's only mouthpiece. I can understand why he felt blessed and wanted to thank God for the people of the church in Rome. I'm sure it encouraged them to keep up the good work as they learned of Paul's thanksgiving. I'm sure that as he thanked God he prayed that they would continue to share their faith.

Similarly, Paul also thanked God for the church at Corinth:

I always thank my God for you because of his grace given you in Christ Jesus. —1 Corinthians. 1:4

The church at Corinth was a mess. No wonder Paul was thankful for grace! The sin there was rampant. Of course, Paul was thankful God had grace to give. He knew who these people were, and he knew they could become something different. It was going to be a work of grace. After all, Paul remembered where he himself had come from. He used to be a rough character—mean and nasty, violent and hateful. He had been arrogant and proud. He had the kind of reputation that made people afraid of him. But God met Paul on the road to Damascus. The Lord humbled him by confronting his horrible behavior, and even physically blinding him, to help him see what he needed to understand and own. That is God's grace at work.

We ought to be thankful for a God who is willing to do whatever it takes to get our attention. It might humble us, it might even hurt us for a minute, but better to receive a time-out from the hand of God in grace than to suffer the consequences of continuing on a path of destruction.

After studying Paul's words, I understand why he could be thankful for a church full of problems. How many pastors are standing in the pulpits of problem-filled churches and are giving thanks? Yet that is the very perspective we ought to have when we pray. Even when we pray for people who are a mess, we can give thanks that there is a way out for them. There is a way up. There is a way forward. There is forgiveness. God doesn't treat us as our sins deserve (Psalm 103:10).

Why is thanksgiving so important? It is an absolute game-changer because it will put our minds in a positive groove. Paul had every reason to go to God in prayer and complain about the church in Corinth. They were difficult. They weren't making great spiritual progress. They were sinning. They were fighting. Services were tense and drama-filled. "Sister So-and-So" didn't speak to "Brother This-and-That"; she only spoke about him when he wasn't around. The worship gatherings weren't God-focused; they were often a chaotic free-for-all. These people had so much to learn. It wasn't an easy church to serve.

If Paul hadn't gotten his mind into a positive place as he prayed for the Corinthian believers, he would never have been able to make a lasting impact on them. He may have wound up praying that God would kick them to the curb. He may have tried to convince God that this church was beyond help. He may have argued with God that Corinth was a lost cause. But he didn't. Because Paul was thankful for God's grace at work in the lives of these believers, he was able to stay invested, to keep working with them, to keep praying for them, to keep believing that something good would come.

You can't make an impact on someone you give up on. People without Christ and those who are newly saved need lots of teaching, nurturing, love, patience, and most of all, prayer. Most people don't change overnight or submit their will overnight. When you pray with thanksgiving, you are acknowledging that God *can* do the seemingly impossible, with impossible people and circumstances. In that respect, to pray with thanksgiving is to pray with great faith. When you pray with thanksgiving you will hang in there with people longer. You will be more willing to listen to them, to work with them, to share life with them.

Knowing Jesus Better

For this reason, ever since I heard about your faith in the Lord Jesus and your love for all God's people, I have not stopped giving thanks for you, remembering you in my prayers. I keep asking that the God of our Lord Jesus Christ, the glorious Father, may give you the Spirit of wisdom and revelation, so that you may know him better. I pray that the eyes of your heart may be enlightened in order that you may know the hope to which he has called you, the riches of his glorious inheritance in his holy people, and his incomparably great power for us who believe. —Ephesians 1:15–19a

Ephesus was the home of the Greek goddess Artemis, also known as Diana. Many people there worshiped her. It was tough to be a Christian and grow as a Christian in Ephesus. Paul prayed that the believers there would know Christ better through the Holy Spirit. What a lasting-impact kind of prayer! Knowing Jesus is critical if you are ever going to know anything else correctly. Without knowing him, you can't find the right way, know the full truth, or have real life (John 14:6).

Knowing Christ better is the result of cultivating a relationship with him. A relationship with Jesus will nurture and sustain us, guide and correct us, challenge and change us. It is ultimately Christ who makes a lasting impact in our lives.

Knowing Christ is also critical because as you learn to know him more, you will uncover more about the inheritance he has for you. You will also come to know yourself better as a result of being in intimate relationship with Jesus.

Paul prayed that the Ephesians would know what God hoped for them to experience, that they would discover all that God had for them on their journey with Christ. Knowing the hope God has called us to is crucial. Each one of us has a specific journey to travel. Abundant life for you might look different than abundant life for me. Just as parents have hopes and dreams for their children, so God has hopes and dreams for each one of us. He wants us to get it all, see it all, and experience it all because it is and will be a life of satisfaction, contentment, and joy like no other.

Paul prayed that the Ephesians would know God's power in their lives as they followed Christ. Why did they need power? Because they had an inheritance in Christ. They needed power to be able to safeguard that inheritance from the Enemy who wanted to rob them.

Spiritual Warfare

Satan doesn't want God's people to inherit anything. He wants them spiritually bankrupt. You may not have much sitting in your bank account this minute, but you have an inheritance in Christ that is priceless. You have salvation through the forgiveness of your sins. You have peace with God, and therefore you can have peace of mind. You have the promises of God and the presence of God to escort you through life. You have a mansion that has been prepared for you in heaven. You are wealthy beyond comprehension! And Satan wants to rob you of that inheritance, of your salvation, and of the eternal retirement plan that God has ordained for those who love him.

Ephesians 6:10–17 tells us about the spiritual battle that is being waged. Paul prayed that the Ephesians would have the power of God to safeguard their inheritance in Christ. He prayed that what the believers at Ephesus already possessed in faith and what they were pursuing would be safeguarded by God's power. It didn't matter what was happening in the temple of the goddess Diana. It didn't matter what the world said was the way to gain happiness and contentment. All that mattered was knowing God, learning what life with him included, and utilizing his power along the way to keep Satan from derailing their pursuit.

Paul prayed for spiritual power for the Ephesians to keep them on the right track. What a lasting mark—how practical, profound, and powerful! We must have strength. We must have power. Otherwise, we become weak and vulnerable to the attack of Satan. Do you want to leave a lasting impact? Pray for your family and friends to know Christ better, to fully know God's hopes for their lives, and to know God's power at work to keep them safe along the way.

Abounding in Love

This is my prayer: that your love may abound more and more in knowledge and depth of insight, so that you may be able to discern what is best and may be pure and blameless for the day of Christ, filled with the fruit of righteousness that comes through Jesus Christ—to the glory and praise of God. —Philippians 1:9–11

I love the phrase "more and more" in regard to love. The more in love we are with Jesus, the more we comprehend how great his love for us is, and the more our own love will increase for God's Word, God's people, and the world. Paul prayed that the Philippian Christians would live a life of increasing love. Why? Because love leaves a lasting mark. It is enduring. It never fails (1 Corinthians 13:8a).

I pray that my children will show love and kindness to all people regardless of their nationality, religious faith, skin color, economic background, social prowess, academic ability, musical skills, or athletic agility. I pray they will love people who are completely different from them. I pray they will love people they haven't even met yet. Why? Because it is the love of God that will impress and transform this culture.

I believe that at the heart of sin is a desire for control—notice that "I" is right in the middle of the word *sin!* We want to be in charge. But another issue at the heart of sin is a desire to be loved. *Can't someone just accept me for who I am? Can't someone just take me "as-is," without strings attached? Can't someone love me where I am?* That's what the world wants to know, and they are pursuing all kinds of sinful, destructive avenues in order to find out.

There is only one person who loves perfectly, and that is Jesus. If anyone should get this right, it ought to be the church. Religion holds up hoops for people to jump through, while love tears down walls and builds bridges for people to walk across. No wonder Paul prayed that the believers' love would increase.

Increasing in Discernment

Paul also prayed that the Philippians would be able to discern what was "best and...pure and blameless" (v 10) until Christ called them home. He prayed for them to grow in discernment. Why? Because we can't do right without knowing right.

I pray that, when faced with temptations and challenges, my children will see Satan's smokescreens. I pray they will be wise to his traps. I pray they will see what the consequences could be for irrational, impulsive, or emotional behavior. Our sense of right and wrong must be constantly sharpened by the Word and Spirit of God because the messages of the world have amazing power to dull our spiritual sensitivities every day.

I believe Satan's favorite color is gray. It's gray because if he can convince you something is a gray area, he can get you to compromise. And once he gets his hooks in you, he will steal your inheritance and make you his slave by making you a slave to sin. We must avoid the blackness of sin, but the slippery slope of grayness is just as dangerous.

Do you want to leave a lasting mark? Pray for your friends to grow in love and discernment.

I pray that your partnership with us in the faith may be effective in deepening your understanding of every good thing we share for the sake of Christ. —Philemon 6

Paul was concerned about the process of discipleship in people's lives. After he prayed for people to know Christ better and to understand what God's hopes and dreams were for them, and once they were armed with God's power and had love for others and discernment, it would only be natural for them to want to share their faith. Spiritual reproduction is our goal. Christians, we need to be having spiritual babies. Wouldn't it be wonderful to see salvations every Sunday in our churches?

———

When people need encouragement, pray for that. When they need a job, pray for that. When they need a physical healing, by all means pray for that. But the truth is that after people are encouraged, it is almost certain they will become discouraged again. After they get a job, there will most certainly be a need for provision again at some point. People who get healed will deal with sickness again as long as they are in a physical body. Perhaps we could say that when these prayers get answered, the results are temporary—necessary, but temporary.

So, in addition to praying these much-needed prayers, pray the kinds of prayers Paul prayed: for the development of people's relationship with Jesus, for an increase in their love and discernment, for people to share their faith and see more people won to the Kingdom. These kinds of prayers, when the answers come, will leave a lasting impact.

10. Training for Maximum Impact:
Preparing to Leave a Mark

Have nothing to do with godless myths and old wives' tales; rather, train yourself to be godly. For physical training is of some value, but godliness has value for all things, holding promise for both the present life and the life to come. This is a trustworthy saying that deserves full acceptance. That is why we labor and strive, because we have put our hope in the living God, who is the Savior of all people, and especially of those who believe.

Command and teach these things. Don't let anyone look down on you because you are young, but set an example for the believers in speech, in conduct, in love, in faith and in purity. Until I come, devote yourself to the public reading of Scripture, to preaching and to teaching. Do not neglect your gift, which was given you through prophecy when the body of elders laid their hands on you.

Be diligent in these matters; give yourself wholly to them, so that everyone may see your progress. Watch your life and doctrine closely. Persevere in them, because if you do, you will save both yourself and your hearers. —1 Timothy 4:7–16

Football is complicated, at least from where I sit. Here's the simplest explanation I have heard. It involves two teams, a fully inflated ball, and an end zone. The goal is to get the ball to the end zone as many times as possible (preferably more than the other team). That's it, right? Yes, but it's about so much more than just game day. Success at football is an ongoing venture. It involves constant training. It is grueling, mentally. It is rigorous, physically. It is a daily commitment to do what it takes to make an impact on the field on the day of the big game. Even the down time that professional athletes spend has purpose and intention. They view every day as preparation day for the next big day. Training, discipline, getting in top shape, developing a winning strategy, and being generally prepared so that you will be ready to impact the outcome of the game—that's what football is all about.

The Apostle Paul wrote 1 Timothy to help his young protégé pastor the church in Ephesus. With its bustling population of 350,000, Ephesus was huge in first-century terms. If ever there was a city that needed a strong church with a strong pastor, it was Ephesus.

The temple of Artemis, the goddess of the Ephesians, was one of the seven wonders of the ancient world. Worship of Artemis was focused on prosperity. Change was a constant in Ephesus, as it was a melting pot of cultures. It had a Greek heritage, but Romans made their way there when it became part of the Roman Empire. There was also a decent-sized Jewish community and a mix of other ethnic groups.

Sports were huge in Ephesus. There were all sorts of gymnasiums that had been built for Greek athletic contests, and a stadium that had been designed by the Romans for gladiator combat. Eventually, the violent and bloody Roman battles became the most popular sport.

Sex was a huge part of the economy in Ephesus. Art was about sex. Commerce was about sex. Various sexual perversions were celebrated. The Romans established a kind of ancient country club where upper-class members of both sexes would bathe or swim in the nude. Prostitution was rampant. Divorce was common, and multiple marriages were routine. Abandoning children and neglecting the elderly were commonplace.

Many religions got mixed into Artemis worship. Many citizens became preoccupied with magic. People in Ephesus were all about deal-making, which had a negative effect on spirituality and religion. It promoted compromise and manipulation.

Paul saw Ephesus as a great place for the good news of the gospel. He preached there a lot, and it made a huge impact on the culture. The practice of magic and the deal-making in the temple took a nose dive as a result of the gospel message going forward. As Paul was preparing to leave the Ephesian church in the pastoral care of Timothy, he had instructions. Victories won would need to be maintained, and many more victories needed to be won. If Timothy and the Christians in Ephesus were going to continue to have an impact there, they needed to follow Paul's instructions regarding ongoing training.

Paul encouraged Timothy and the church to train their heads, their hearts, and their whole lives in order to have a maximum Kingdom impact. Appealing to their love for athletics, he wrote about how physical training is beneficial, but there was another kind of training that would serve God's people in this life and in the life to come—a kind of training that each of us needs to be most focused on. We shouldn't skip walking, aerobics, or weight lifting, but we should make sure our spiritual training is a priority.

Training Our Heads

To train for maximum impact, we need to train our minds to believe and live by the truth of God's Word. There are a lot of things in this world we can study. There are ideas bombarding us constantly. There is no shortage of philosophies seeking to consume our mental energy. What we decide to open our minds to can affect our training for maximum impact. A winning strategy will include mental focus, which also means excluding unhelpful thoughts.

Paul warned Timothy (and us) to "have nothing to do with godless myths and old wives' tales" (v 7a). And something else was problematic in Ephesus (see 1 Timothy 1). People were teaching false doctrines and getting wrapped up in genealogies, which promoted controversy rather than the work of God.

Myths...wives' tales...false doctrines...genealogies. Attention to these kinds of things starts early, doesn't it? Step on a crack and break your mother's back. Find a penny, pick it up; all day long you'll have good luck. Have you heard the old superstition that death seems to come in threes? Or how about the one where you aren't supposed to breathe when you go past a cemetery because you may breathe in the spirit of someone who has recently departed? Have you embraced the notion that Friday the 13th is a bad or cursed day?

We have bought these wives' tales and lies hook, line, and sinker. Were you told not to cross your eyes as a kid because they would get stuck that way? Did you know that swallowing gum won't really hurt your digestive system, and it won't take seven years to digest? or that cracking your knuckles won't really cause arthritis? or that you don't really have to wait an hour after eating before swimming?

Hanging a horseshoe over your door won't bring you good luck. Making a wish before blowing out candles or wishing on a star won't make the wish come true. Knocking on wood and keeping your fingers crossed will only hurt your hand. A watched pot will still boil, and the lines in your palm say nothing about the number of children you will have or what your future will look like. You didn't have a past life, you won't be reincarnated, and there is no such thing as karma or "good energy."

And I want to mention one more popular form of superstition that is floating around out there on the Internet: posting something that says, "If you aren't ashamed of Jesus, share this or post it on your page." Sometimes this is accompanied by the suggestion that you must forward the post to ten people in ten minutes to receive a blessing. This is not a way to encourage people or a way through which people receive God's blessing. It is a form of superstition and manipulation, and it isn't something Christians should be promoting. Our faith isn't in a chain letter passed along by a well-meaning friend. It is in a dynamic, ongoing relationship with Jesus Christ.

Did you know that Mormonism is based entirely on myths about early history in America that can't be supported one iota by archaeology or other evidence? The Book of Mormon is a book of myths. Mormon people are some of the finest, most moral, and most upstanding people anywhere, but they are deceived.

The genealogies Paul was writing about dealt with the Jewish tradition of keeping strict records of their bloodlines, tracing their heritage and their ties to one of the twelve tribes. The whole thing had become way too important to the Jews. They had kept records to try to identify the Messiah in their heritage. But now that the Messiah had come, they were to cease keeping themselves distinct from other nations. Paul said the genealogies were endless, unnecessary, and promoting conflict.

So, if these things aren't to be occupying our minds, what should be? Reading God's Word, preaching, and teaching. If there is one thing you can't go overboard with, it is the Word of God. The Bible says that if you meditate on it day and night, your life will be firmly established as a result (Psalm 1). It's impossible to get too much of the Scriptures.

Training Our Hearts

In order to train for maximum impact, we also need to train our hearts to hope in Christ alone. We have put our hope in the living God. Your hope cannot be in people who will disappoint you. Your hope cannot be in your health, because everyone will grow weaker and deal with the complications that come from living in an earthly body. Your hope cannot be found in your good looks, because beauty is fleeting. Your hope cannot be found in your networks, because people will turn on you in an instant. Your hope cannot be found in your paycheck, because it could be gone tomorrow. Your hope cannot be found in the acquisition of things, because they are only temporary and can be repossessed, burned in a fire, or sold when economic times get tough.

"On Christ, the solid Rock, I stand; All other ground is sinking sand, All other ground is sinking sand."[3] Christ needs to be our source of hope. This means that when the unexpected or unwanted happens, he is the *first* place we go. It is to Jesus that we should go first, because he has the ability to impact how the tough times will play out. I'd rather have Jesus guiding me through a bad situation from the beginning than wait until I am in the middle of the deep waters to call upon his name. Why should I get myself emotionally and physically off kilter trying to keep myself afloat in the deep, when I can let him carry me through it all from the beginning of the storm?

Having hope in Christ means living in a constantly blessed state. Because I am never without hope, I am blessed. Hope takes me forward. Hope fuels my faith, and faith fuels my hope. Hope helps me see God's promises the way he intends. Hope keeps me praying. Hope keeps me connected to the body of Christ in my church, where I can get help. Hope keeps me from giving up. Hope gives me peace in my mind and my heart. If you have nothing the world would call important today, but you have hope, you are blessed and highly favored. Place your hope securely in Christ, knowing that he won't disappoint you.

Training Our Lives

Finally, to train for maximum impact, we need to train our whole lives as an example for others. First Timothy 4:12 is the theme verse for the youth ministry at our church:

Don't let anyone look down on you because you are young, but set an example for the believers in speech, in conduct, in love, in faith and in purity.

3   Edward Mote, "The Solid Rock," *from Worship the Lord: Hymnal of the Church of God* (Anderson, IN: Warner Press, 1989), 420.

Regardless of our age, we need to be training to become the kind of person others can look up to as they follow Christ.

There are moments in every sports competition when the officials will make calls that are obvious, cut and dried. They are so clearly seen by everyone watching that the game will go forward without much commentary. There will be other calls, however, that cause a great reaction. Some people will cheer, and others will boo. Some calls will be discussed, criticized, or argued by commentators because they are so close they could go either way. The decision won't be clear; it will be disputable. There will be room to question what really happened.

Paul told Timothy to press forward in these things so others would see. In other words, he was to train so that people could clearly see how far he had come. If we once were lost and now we are found, we need to make sure we are living like found persons, not lost persons.

Swearing, perversion, and gossip might flow from the lips of a lost person. This person might be negative, critical, and angry. But such language and attitudes ought not characterize the life of a found person. Our words should be instructional, helpful, seasoned with salt from the Word, and reflecting only that which is true and worthy of being presented or repeated.

Lost people may live for the moment, seeking the applause of others, striving to feel good or acquire things. But those ideals ought not characterize the life of a found person who is devoted to Christ alone and to making Christ known.

Lost people may live for love based on the world's definition, focused on lust and gratification, manipulation and self-satisfaction. Those worldly ideas of love are transformed in the life of a found person, who begins to embrace a love that is patient and kind and sacrificial, never jealous or rude, never self-seeking or record keeping (1 Corinthians 13).

Lost people may view faith as a crutch, something to lean on just to get by for a season, or even a hindrance to being happy in the now. But found people know that faith isn't merely a belief; it is a pattern for living that connects us to the dynamic, powerful, life-giving, life-changing presence of the Almighty God who makes a home in all who are willing to receive him. This not only affects the now but also impacts eternity.

What about lost people and purity? I wouldn't expect them to view purity as important. If there is no relationship with God, then there isn't a moral standard for a person to follow. Purity? What is that to a lost person? A way of life that keeps you from having fun, or an outdated idea that makes dating difficult and complicated. But found people know that the best possible expression of sexuality is within the boundaries God has ordained in a marriage between a man and a woman. Found people learn that our bodies are temples of the living God, so God does have a say in how they are used. Found people know that sexual intimacy is best cultivated within the marriage relationship.

Paul's words encourage us to strive to become a Christian example of what it means to live for God in speech, conduct, love, faith, and purity. In every area of life, we should strive to leave no room for doubt. Don't let it be a close call. Don't be so close to the line in your speech, in your love, in your purity, or in any area that others question if you are the real deal—*you might be a Christian, but on the other hand you might not be.* Instead, let your life speak so clearly that if people want to follow Christ, they don't have to wonder whether following you would lead them closer to that desire.

I don't know a lot of Christians who willfully set out to sin, but I do know a lot of Christians who allow compromise into their lives, which leads to sin. When we compromise, our consciences become desensitized to sin, and sinning becomes more of a natural inclination than holiness does. You see, Satan doesn't have to get Christians to sin (at first)—he just has to get them to compromise. No one who embraces compromise becomes the kind of example Paul urged Timothy and his church to become.

———

Why are these three areas of training so important? Because lives are at stake. Your example could lead to the salvation of others, which would make you a person of great impact.

A story is told about Louis Pasteur, the pioneer of immunology, who lived at a time when thousands of people died annually from rabies. Pasteur had worked for years on a vaccine. Just as he was about to begin experimenting on himself, a nine-year-old boy named Joseph Meister was bitten by a rabid dog. The boy's mother begged Pasteur to experiment on her son. Pasteur injected Joseph for ten days—and the boy lived. Decades later, of all the things Pasteur could have had etched on his headstone, he asked for three words: JOSEPH MEISTER LIVED.

Our greatest legacy will be those who live eternally because of our efforts. It's not just about making it to heaven ourselves, but about helping as many others as possible get there as well. Living to make an impact requires that we train our heads, our hearts, and our whole lives to reveal to other people who Jesus really is.

We are therefore Christ's ambassadors, as though God were making his appeal through us. —2 Corinthians 5:20a

As you close the pages of this book, I encourage you to offer a prayer asking God to help you impact your community in a way that forever marks them with the love, grace, and forgiveness that comes through Jesus Christ. Let's leave a lasting mark for the glory of God!

Discussion Questions

Chapter 1
Impact: Colliding with the Culture

1. Who has made a positive and lasting impact on your life? How have your interactions with this person shaped you?

2. In what ways do you think the church is being impacted by the culture?

3. How might you alter your weekly routine so that you can "run into others on purpose"?

Chapter 2
A Collective Impact: The Mark of the Church

1. In what ways are we better together as believers when it comes to making an impact?

2. How can your participation in a local body of believers add to the overall impact of that church?

3. Do you welcome instruction and discipline into your life? Why or why not?

4. How does your church celebrate what happens in the lives of its people?

Chapter 3
A Gospel Impact: Living the Transformed Life

1. How does your life reflect that the gospel is "good news"?

2. How does the way you handle disappointment and pain make an impact on those around you?

3. Are you walking in freedom, or are you struggling with an addiction or some other form of bondage?

4. How committed are you to living well, growing in Christ, and finishing strong?

5. What broken walls and devastated places are you giving of yourself in order to rebuild?

Chapter 4
Words of Impact: The Power of Your Story

1. Who has impacted your life by sharing his or her personal salvation story?

2. With whom, and in what ways, are you actively sharing your testimony? If you have trouble answering this question, perhaps consider writing your story down and praying for God to show you how you can make an impact on someone by sharing that story.

Chapter 5
A Courageous Impact: Stepping Up and Out in Faith

1. In what situations has God used you to help people find life and liberation?

2. When have you felt overwhelming concern and compassion for others? How has God used you in those situations to meet needs?

3. Who has supported and encouraged you when others doubted your ability? What difference did it make?

4. Recall a time you had to step up and lead. What impact did your courage have on the situation?

5. When was the last time you were vulnerable enough with God or others to confess sin or a need for help? What was the outcome?

Chapter 6
Attitudes that Impact: Adopting the Attitude of Jesus

1. How could being silent have a negative impact? How could it have a positive impact?

2. How could generosity and grace translate into Kingdom impact in someone's life?

3. When is it most difficult for you to have a positive attitude?

4. What would you have to change in order to have the attitude of Christ?

Chapter 7
A Generational Impact: Inspiring Faith in Others

1. Who are the younger people who are watching your life? How is your faith, commitment to Christ, and attitude impacting them to follow Christ more faithfully?

2. Do you have a passion for Kingdom living that includes serving, worshipping, witnessing, praying, and giving in ways that encourage the next generation to live in a similar fashion?

3. Are you spending time in fellowship with members of the next generation and teaching them the truths of God's Word?

4. Is your life characterized by a positive confession and regular testimony to God's goodness?

Chapter 8
An Everywhere Impact: An Evangelism Lifestyle

1. On what hard, rocky, or thorny path have you scattered the seed of the gospel? What was the outcome?

2. What has it cost you personally in order to witness to someone about Christ?

3. In what ways are you engaging the culture—right where people are—in an effort to share about Jesus?

4. How can you use your own life experiences to connect with those who are experiencing similar struggles?

5. How can you equip yourself to more effectively share the gospel with others?

6. With whom can you begin a conversation about Jesus?

Chapter 9
A Prayerful Impact: A Strategy for Transformation

1. Who is on your current prayer list? How can you let them know you are praying for them?

2. How can God shape you through the ministry of prayer to be more passionate about sharing his love with others?

3. How can you become more strategic in your prayers for others in order to impact them for Christ?

Chapter 10
Training for Maximum Impact: Preparing to Leave a Mark

1. What kind of regular spiritual training are you undergoing to prepare you for maximum impact?

2. What things might need to be eliminated from your life to enable you to make an eternal difference in someone else's life?

3. Is your life characterized by hope, peace, faith, and victory? If not, what changes can you make to exhibit that kind of witness?

4. Are there any "gray areas" in your life that could cause people to question your commitment to Christ?

5. What is God calling you to do as a result of reading this book?